FIGHTING TO GIVE

The Jimmy Culveyhouse Story

HEATHER
Thanks for your
hard work with our
team. You are a classy
lady. Hope you enjoy the
book. 100% of THE research
proceeds will go To research
God BLESS
Chris 6/23/09

By: amazon.com

CHRISTOPHER STEVENS

www.fightingtogive.com
617 510 5028

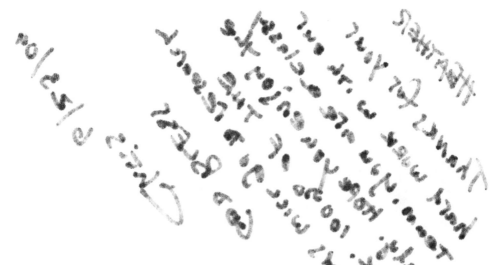

ISBN: 1-4392-3075-7
ISBN13: 9781439230756
LCCN: 2009901863

Visit www.booksurge.com to order additional copies

This book represents the life of Jimmy Culveyhouse as told to the author by Jimmy, his friends and family members. The representation of the facts presented herein have been approved and verified by Jimmy.

DEDICATION

Dedicated to Jimmy, his family and friends, and all those who are fighting to give of themselves to raise money for research for currently incurable diseases

To the loved ones my family has lost and to all of the friends and family members who won't be able to enjoy their golden years

To all of Jimmy's friends and family members
who contributed to this book
Thanks to Frank Murnane for his editing
To John Rizzo, Abby & the BookSurge team for believing
Thanks to Brian Zimmerman and Crea843.com,
who designed the book cover and interior
Jenny you are an amazing editor
To the readers: Forgive me,
I'm no writer – just telling Jimmy's story

CONTENTS

The First Tee

The Irish Guard stomped their feet in a rhythmic march, knees held high as they cleared the way for the country's oldest college marching band.

It was an impressive sight. The Guard boasted ten students, all of whom stood at least six-foot-two, and many of whom were high school sports stars with "Rudy-like" dreams of playing for the Fighting Irish in their preferred sport. Their uniforms sparkled brightly beneath an azure autumn sky. In their Scottish kilts, incorporating the unique Notre Dame tartan, they were regal in appearance. Adorned with the distinguished shakos atop their heads elevating their height to eight feet tall, they commanded the respect and admiration of all on campus.

Originally formed in 1949, they marched in a line as straight as any ever plumbed by a master carpenter as they served as the protectorate for the mass of demure flutists, clarinet players, and accompanying brass and percussion players: the band of the Fighting Irish of Notre Dame.

Having successfully negotiated the gauntlet of the North Quad's finest early morning revelers, they steered past historic Edwards Hall into the shadow of the revered Administration Building, which bragged as its most glamorous feature the infamous Golden Dome. Atop this glistening magnificence, a gilded facsimile of founder Father Sorin stood erect and peered down approvingly on his favored sons and daughters. The band marched past, beneath a sky so stunning it looked more purple than blue. Foster Grants or other protective eyewear was required for extended viewing.

Airfare: $350. A room at the Morris Inn on campus: $240. Two tickets on the forty-yard line: $128. Walking the campus with a cold one, hearing the "Notre Dame Fight Song" on a crisp October morn: priceless.

As the Irish Guard created a path for the band, the ensemble cleared Walsh Hall and rounded the corner on its way to the historic South Quad. A smile erupted on the face of a frail man who sat unnoticed by the mass who followed the music.

Propped on a bench beneath a sprawling maple, the diminutive Notre Dame alum nodded approvingly, having been witness to this wonderful pageantry so many times before. As the band's music faded away, he tilted his head back to allow the watery eyes behind the tinted frames to once again gaze upon the image of Notre Dame's founding father. Tears flowed freely, cascading down his cheeks onto the ND monogram patch on his left chest.

The jacket, symbolic of varsity athletic achievement at this storied university, rarely was worn by a man of such short stature. But this was no ordinary honoree who proudly wore the striking garment. While standing only five-foot-six, he had earned four of these letters as a golfer in the mid-1970s. The coat, the likes of which had also warmed the chiseled frames of legends like Rockne, Gipp, Paul Hornung, and Joe Montana, welcomed the tears of this loving, modest man, for he also was a man worthy of acclaim. He too was a "son of Notre Dame."

As he soaked in the sight of the shining, freshly renovated Golden Dome, he knew it was a sight he never tired of viewing. He also knew he would never see it again. He had gazed lovingly upon it at least fifty times on preceding weekends the past thirty years but it always evoked the same sense of pride. Some pilgrims seek their inner peace with an annual journey to Mecca. For this man, it was here that he felt most at home. Among all the wonders of the world he could have enjoyed on his last trip he would ever take, he chose Notre Dame… and there was no second option.

The end was near. There would be no more pilgrimages from his home to South Bend, no more trips from the misty capital city of Oregon, three time zones removed. This was his final voyage. What began improbably thirty years ago from the sooty skyline of Gary, Indiana, could end here today, and the conclusion to this tortuous chapter of his amazing life would be idyllic.

As he struggled to catch his breath, he was struck by the irony of the moment. He was never happier in any other locale, but he also knew it could not end here. Despite his fragile state, there was a football game to see, work to do, more he had left to give to those he loved, and more money to raise to help find a cure.

He gathered his composure, strained to muster some strength, and then turned his head toward the South Quad.

There she was, as she had been every day of this journey, smiling approvingly at him, allowing him to enjoy this moment that he had traveled two thousand miles to experience. Patient enough to not interrupt the moment, and wise enough to monitor his every move, with a concern undetected to the human eye, she was his guardian angel. But unlike most angels, she was there in plain view for the entire world to see – and for him to cherish.

"You doin' OK, Jim?" she whispered tenderly.

"No problem," he responded with a pronounced slur.

So many times he had been the show, dominated the stage, was the life of the party, the one who injected energy into any situation. But now, relegated to an incapacitated state at the relatively young age of fifty-four, Jimmy Culveyhouse was tired, but he was content. He adored his beloved Melanie, without whom he could not do. And his faith in his Lord had never been stronger. He knew his time was limited and he knew his affliction was incurable. But he was at peace. He was home. For the first time he could remember, he stopped thinking of others and just basked in the moment.

Before he struggled to rise, Jim reflected on three of his favorite books. The first was *Rudy*, the inspirational true story about one of his classmates, a walk-on football player at Notre Dame, Rudy Ruettiger. He also thought about Mitch Albom's wonderful tribute to one of his college professors, Morrie Schwartz, in the book *Tuesdays With Morrie*. And finally, John Feinstein's moving portrait of the life of Tom Watson's longtime PGA caddie, Bruce Edwards. Jim smiled, marveling at the fact that his life seemed to embody an amazing combination of all three of these stories.

Passersby who noticed did so fleetingly as if he was some kind of leper. Listing noticeably as he struggled to walk, his head bobbing up and down, with drool often dribbling down his mouth, he could not walk unassisted. Jimmy was used to the stares by now. Ignoring them, he reflected that the pride he felt in his heart was not related to his accomplishments, which were truly extraordinary, but rather from what he knew he had given to others during the last few years of his life. Someone once said, "Good things come in small packages." Jimmy Culveyhouse embodied that sentiment as much as anyone.

He was an ordinary man with an extraordinary amount of determination. In fact, as he walked, something extraordinary occurred. At first, she didn't notice. They reached the middle of the South Quad where Jim always liked to stand and soak up the wonder that was Notre Dame. He could turn around in circles and see the Golden Dome, then ninety degrees to the right where he could see the classrooms of O'Shaughnessy Hall. Further in the distance, the Hesburgh Library loomed over the North Quad with its famous mural "Touchdown Jesus" blessing all the Fighting Irish who did battle in Notre Dame Stadium.

Then, a ninety-degree turn to the right and he was peering at the beautiful walkway that greeted visitors near the entrance of Notre Dame. Flanked by the Law School on the left and Alumni Hall on the right, the entrance had changed a lot over the years to accommodate the ever evolving needs of campus life.

Finally, he completed the last rotation and gazed down the South Quad to the storied Rockne Gymnasium, behind which stood the site of his greatest athletic accomplishment. Named for the legendary football coach Knute Rockne, the "Rock" was where the golf team housed its lockers. But in the actual competitive courts of the Rock, so many "walk-ons" lived out their fantasies, playing inter-hall sports at Notre Dame.

While Jim usually would complete this ritual of revolutions several times, something dramatic happened. Traditionally, at the conclusion of this regimen, he would grab Melanie's arm and start to head over to the football stadium to see his beloved Irish tend to battle. This would be the last time to do it and Melanie's arm was outstretched to offer the assistance which would be required to complete this final labor of love.

But instead of heading toward the stadium, he began to walk toward the Rock. After the first few paces, Melanie started to follow him. She was uncertain what to do but she would give him a lot of latitude on this nostalgic final trip to South Bend.

Suddenly, the amazing occurred. His pace quickened for the first time in months.

"What are you doing, Jim?" blurted out his surprised wife. "How can you walk that fast?" She paused. "Jim, honey... I am worried."

With each stride more pronounced than the one prior and his posture becoming more erect, he seemed like Forest Gump. Just as Forest broke out of his braces and began to run when he was being chased by bullies, Jim felt the same kind of supernatural energy as he laid his head back and responded clearly:

"No problem."

What? Jim had not uttered a phrase clearly in more than eighteen months. *What was going on here?* Melanie thought.

A quickened pace suddenly turned into a rapid one and then yielded to a slow trot. As improbable as Robert DeNiro rising bright-eyed and bushy-tailed after years in a coma in the movie *The Awakening,* Jim Culveyhouse was doing the unthinkable. Tears of joy streaked down his cheeks as onlookers on the South Quad began to notice this withered old man with the spirit and speed of a wingback. He streaked past the Rockne Gym yelling to Melanie, "Try to keep up... I will meet you at the first tee!"

Melanie was so shocked she was trembling as she fruitlessly tried to keep pace. The only words she heard from her sprinting spouse were "the first tee." She slowed down and, while not yet understanding what was taking place before her eyes, she instantly knew where she would find him.

The first tee of the golf course of the University of Notre Dame sits just yards from the rear of the Rock. Melanie arrived at the first tee totally breathless. But when she saw him she burst into tears. There he was, at the site of his historic achievement.

Like the undersized Rudy who walked onto the Notre Dame football team and actually ended up getting into a game, Jimmy Culveyhouse had enjoyed the same kind of athletic epiphany. But Jimmy's would stand forever, not just as an appearance, but as milestone no one else would ever achieve – or could ever achieve.

Jimmy Culveyhouse was standing in the very spot where he made history more than thirty years before when he set the course record at Notre Dame with a blistering score of sixty-four. It would be a record which would stand forever as testimony to the skills of this over-achieving little man. It would never be broken because, due to the need to expand housing and create new classroom buildings, nine holes had been usurped by the administration. His eighteen-hole record score would stand the test of time, for only nine holes remained of what used to be a wonderfully challenging campus golf course, the Burke Memorial Golf Course.

The plaque which memorialized his score still stood proudly for all to see. Some old timers who had been getting ready to tee it up had stepped aside. They were bearing witness with the same sense of awe which befell Melanie and others nearby.

Jim surveyed the course as if he was Kevin Costner gazing upon the corn field baseball diamond in that wonderful movie *Field of Dreams*. The whispers of "Build it and they will come" came to mind.

But there was Jimmy standing there with a tee and a Titlist golf ball cupped in his small hand. With one swift motion, he planted the tee in the ground with the ball properly seated in it. Armed with his faithful old Ben Hogan persimmon three-wood, he was about to address the ball.

Melanie was in shock as it was not a frail, diseased tired man she saw standing there. It was the man she married. No – it was a younger man. It was her husband as a twenty-year-old. This could not be happening. Without even a practice swing, the young man they called "Stump" steadily and gracefully drew the wood back and with a follow-through that brought images of Tom Watson to mind, the ball exploded off the tee, arching with a gentle draw down the fairway. It would come to rest some 280 yards out.

Jimmy froze his follow-through and closed his eyes. He didn't need to see where his majestic drive landed. He knew it was good. He just soaked up the moment and smiled. And just as he...

"Dad, wake up. Dad... hey... wake up, you're crying in your sleep again."

The words hit me like a jolt of lightening. My eyes opened laboriously and I bolted up from the couch, almost knocking my laptop off the glass tabletop.

"Dad... you OK?"

"You have to be kidding me," I uttered, and as I reoriented myself, I realized – it was just a dream. Even my daughter Riley talking to me was not real. There I was on a Sunday afternoon, alone, drool on the side of my cheek, with just my thoughts to keep me company.

I wasn't invisibly bearing witness to this wonderful transformation. Melanie wasn't still panting hard trying to catch her breath, and my friend Jimmy Culveyhouse wasn't frozen in a follow-through on the first tee at Notre Dame. It was just a dream. Just one of those dreams that when you are in it, you swear, as bizarre as the circumstances are, you are living it live.

I have had a lot of dreams lately and Jimmy has been in a few, but none as vivid as this one. I am sure a shrink would have a field day with it. Maybe it is just my hope for Jimmy. The last four years of his life have been hell.

What a Ride

Confucius said, "Choose a job you love and you never have to work a day in your life."

Someone else once added, "Pursue what you love and the money will follow."

"Do not dwell in the past, do not dream in the future. Concentrate the mind on the present moment"- Buddha

Lou Holtz stated, "When all is said and done, more is said than done."

How about Vince Lombardi? "The quality of a man's life is in direct proportion to his commitment to excellence, regardless of his chosen field of endeavor."

"Do not let what you cannot do interfere with what you can do."- John Wooden

I wish I could remember who wisely observed that "Business is like golf: it's the follow through that counts"

"Do not squander time, for that is what life is made of." – Carl Sandburg

"A good friend is one who walks through the door when the rest of the world walks out." I saw that one on the desk of an old boss.

"Life should not be a journey to the grave with the intention of arriving safely in an attractive and well-preserved body, but rather to skid sideways, chocolate in one hand, martini in the other, body thoroughly used up, totally worn out and screaming 'woohoo, what a ride!'"

I love quotes and I use them all the time, attempting to give due credit to those who first uttered them, always ruing the fact I did not think of them first. There is something about a good quote that I just love. All of the above quotes I can roll off my tongue, on demand, or when a particular situation stimulates the thought. All of them, that is, except the last one. That one I saw at 4:45 a.m. one early morning in July 2008 just as I was exiting a lovely home on Pawnee Circle in Salem, Oregon.

Ironically, I have thought about all of the first ten quotes over the past few months (and more) and I've been able to apply them in one way or another to the friend about whose life this book is being written. But there are no words which better describe his life and how he has lived it then those in the last quote.

Jimmy partied hard and lived the first fifty years of his life at full speed. But, sadly, his epitaph is being written. He is not only on the back nine of his life. He is coming down the eighteenth fairway. I've got to get writing because Jimmy's last round is almost over.

A Legacy

I have always been fascinated with the concept of a "legacy." There are several definitions in Webster's Dictionary. But as the years have passed, the importance of the concept seems to be enhanced with each passing birthday.

I am an avid reader of military history as well as sports. As a president nears the end of his term in office, members of the press will invariably speculate as to what will be his legacy. In other words, how will his time in office be defined after he is gone?

For Abraham Lincoln, one might argue it was the Emancipation Proclamation or how he saved the union even at a cost of more than six hundred thousand lives. James K. Polk became known as the "Expansionist President."

Despite more significant accomplishments, unfortunately sometimes a presidency is defined by more negative events. For Herbert Hoover, it was the Great Depression. Or worse, when you think of Richard Nixon, my guess is most people would not opt for his successful initiative to re-open relations with Communist China. More probably, Watergate and his second term resignation would be foremost on most minds.

Bill Clinton? During his two terms in office, we enjoyed eight basically war-free years and our nation feasted on incredible financial prosperity. But my guess is the indiscreet actions which took place in the Oval Office and his subsequent impeachment or images of his happy ending on Monica's dress would be more frequently recalled than his presidential policies.

Someone once said, "Respect is built up through hundreds of positive deeds but destroyed by one stupid one." Integrity retained is invaluable; integrity once lost is irretrievable.

We spend so much of our adult life building a resume of accomplishments and material things we can enjoy. We then hope we leave behind a life in which all our loved ones may take great pride. As we age, the desire to leave a legacy that is positive versus one that is not becomes the focus of many of us middle-aged Americans.

The need to leave an honorable legacy is not limited to politicians or soldiers like General Douglas MacArthur, who said, "I shall return." Athletes wish to be remembered for their great deeds as well. Sometimes it doesn't always turn out as intended. Some stay too long attempting to squeeze out that last ounce of fame and fortune. And some let vice, addiction, or just plain arrogance destroy their legacy. I think of Marion Jones, Pete Rose, Roger Clemens, and Barry Bonds. The jury is still out on the last two but certainly their record achievements within the lines will be forever tarnished by present-day accusations.

Sometimes unexpected circumstances arise which define us. Pat Tillman will little be remembered for his prowess on the gridiron for the Arizona Cardinals. After 9/11, he bid adieu to a multi-million dollar contract so he could join his brother and fight for our country. President Lincoln characterized those who died in battle at Gettysburg as having given "the last full measure of devotion." The apparent victim of "friendly fire" while on active duty in Afghanistan, Pat Tillman did indeed offer up his full measure of devotion and will forever be a hero to anyone with a pulse.

Then, there's you and me and others like us. We just plod away trying to do the right thing. We hope we don't do anything stupid – like Alex Rodriguez was accused of doing in the divorce papers filed by his wife, Cynthia – but rather stay focused on family, friends, and the task at hand. We give to the community and we want to make a difference, a positive difference, and we hope to be remembered for such.

It has been my observation that a life is broken into three sections. The first twenty-five years are spent just figuring it all out. You are born, your folks or guardians give you the tools and try to create an environment where some day you will be able to take care of yourself. You fall down… you get up… you fall down… you get up again. These are life's "potty training years." You don't know squat but you think you know it all.

I think it was Will Rogers Jr. who said something to the effect that when he was sixteen years old his father was the dumbest man in the world. When he was twenty, his dad was the smartest – and wasn't it amazing how intelligent his dad got during those four years?

Most of us live in a virtual cocoon, sheltered from life's harsh realities. Depending on how doting your folks are, you aren't forced to bear life's burdens until after you either start working or you graduate from college. Even then, it still takes a few years to realize that the world does not revolve around you, particularly us guys.

Once having been enlightened, the second trimester of life is about building: a career, a family, and a bank account to sustain you in advanced years. Most dream of creating a legacy of wealth and values we will pass on to our children while we create a nest egg that will allow us to enjoy retirement, whenever that may come. Even if we come from privileged circumstances, we want the same thing: to give our kids or whomever we care about more than what we had when we were younger. We want our legacy to be a lasting positive one which will inspire those we leave behind.

For most husbands, the second trimester of life is more usually a non-stop pressure cooker existence of setting and exceeding objectives. No disrespect to the growing number of other breadwinning spouses or single moms who must do the same thing, but as a dad and father of five, this is how I can best relate.

You do what it takes to make the numbers. You put in the overtime at the mill. You take on a second job. You work for the next promotion. You do this while you try to raise a family or support the church, local town, or other activities designed to define your life.

As Winston Churchill once said, "Don't do your best; do what it takes to get the job done.". The second trimester of life is about getting it done

Then, of course, the pay-off: Phase III, the golden years. Once we turn fifty, our sights are set more on the finish line, on enjoying the fruits of our labor – more time with family or time dedicated to the driving range trying to get the handicap down. These are just a couple of options to be coveted by whatever your passion may be. Walks with grandkids, nieces, and nephews, sharing with them the wisdom you have painfully gained from mistakes too plentiful to count. The "war" stories we share keep those youthful eyes as wide open as saucers. We dial it back a little to try to enjoy the home stretch. Afternoon naps may be enjoyed in the golden years because they have been earned. Years of guilt experienced sneaking these little pleasures yield to willing acceptance.

For those who grew up in the 1950s and 1960s, we had Ozzie and Harriet as TV role models. They were clearly in the third phase of their lives. Apparently, the middle-aged Ozzie had already achieved his goals, because I never remember any episode that showed him as anything other than a financially secure dad sitting around the house in his sweater and slacks. He either was independently wealthy or on a generous disability as he sure seemed financially secure.

His lovely wife, Harriet, was typically perfectly pressed and always seemed to have it together. If Hollywood had a "Stepford" borough, my guess is that Harriet was from there. Their well-adjusted teen sons, David and Ricky Nelson, were the envy of all of us who watched each week. They had home stability, two parents who loved them, financial security, and a seemingly endless amount of time to pursue their passions rather than be slaves to their studies. Many of us watched each week as much out of pure envy, wishing we had lives like that.

Most often, though, it just doesn't work out that way. I don't know about you but little in my life mirrors the one depicted on the set of Ozzie and Harriett. Life after fifty seems a lot harder for many than it rightfully should be. Unforeseen circumstances often interrupt our ride to prosperity. Some people's legacies are cut short before their time, not by choice but by circumstance.

Unfortunately, I know from personal experience. Or, I should say "experiences."

My wife, Marian, worked her entire life to be able to enjoy her children when she grew older. She was the daughter of a south-side Chicago Irishman who pushed hard to do the best for his four children and loving wife, Marita. Marian's father, Tom McBride Jr., did not live long enough to enjoy his children as adults or the majority of what would eventually be thirteen grandchildren.

Tom died of a heart attack in a restaurant parking lot in Berwyn, Illinois, at the age of fifty-two.

It was his lifestyle, some said, that did him in. A longtime chain smoker, he was an old school salesman. He drove hard, drank hard, didn't exercise and loved his cigarettes. But he was a "closer." And in the business world, co-habitation with a few vices was acceptable – even expected – as long as you got the numbers.

Tom was the son of an Irish immigrant who, according to Tom, came to this country when he was twelve years old smoking Camel cigarettes. Tom's father would live until he was eighty and he smoked right up to the time he died. Young Tom would not be so fortunate.

Always impeccably dressed, Tom McBride worked for the Keyes Fiber paper company, makers of the Chinet plates and other fine quality products. A friend of Ray Kroc, founder of McDonald's Hamburgers, Tom had the McDonald's account and he was as good a salesman as there ever was. He was faithful, hard working, spiritual, and dedicated to his family. He deserved to enjoy the third trimester of his life. He may have had his weaknesses, as we all do. But he was a wonderful provider for his wife and four kids.

Their home at the corner of 93rd and Leavitt on Chicago's Beverly Hills south side was always neat and orderly. He taught his kids well. Sue, Marian, Jeanne, and Thomas III, ("Baby Tom") were children in which Tom and Marita could take great pride. Tom made the sacrifices necessary early on. In the back stretch of his life his plan was to be able to relax and enjoy the grandkids, just like his father had been able to do.

But the years of hard living caught up with Tom. At the age of fifty, he suffered severe chest pains. His young son, Tom, rushed him to the hospital in time for the doctors to save him and he underwent a quadruple by-pass surgery. I will never forget him swearing from his hospital bed that he was so grateful for a second chance and that his long-term affair with cigarettes was over.

After he was released and regained his strength, Tom was back on the job, closing sales and bringing home more bacon for the family. His zest for life returned, but so did his affection for nicotine and cocktails. Before you knew it the practice of sneaking cigarettes yielded to an open return to his usual smoking ways.

On the anniversary of his surgery, his buddies all showed up at his home in hospital gowns with drinks for him, served in bedpans. Tom loved the attention. He would soon forget the oath of abstention from cigarettes and booze that he swore off from his hospital bed.

The grim reaper did not approve. One year later, when he came calling again, his action was decisive and final. Tom McBride would not grow old to enjoy the family he so cherished. His legacy was not what he had in mind. In a parking lot, outside of one of his favorite watering holes, the "only son of an Irish immigrant" met his maker.

While parents often may say, "Don't do as I do, do as I say," if you are from the Beverly section of the south side of Chicago, it is pretty hard not to do as many do, which is to celebrate your Irish-Catholic heritage the old fashioned way, with wonderful gatherings of family and friends and plenty of food, booze, Old Style, and Miller Lite. And always root for the south side–situated White Sox.

While my wife, Marian, could party with the best of them in her early years, she decided to escape the traditions of the south side. When we were married in 1977, we moved to the suburbs of Detroit, then to Cincinnati before finally settling in the Boston area.

Her dad met his fate shortly after we moved to Boston. His death engendered in Marian an epiphany of sorts. When we started our family, there would be no smoking and no more drinking. While no one can say for sure what it was that took her dad from us,

Marian certainly didn't want to take any chances. She would work hard, live right, and raise her kids in a Christian home and try to live a healthy life. Her first fifty years were full of sacrifice and hard work. She earned her right to quality time with family and friends. Her friends adored her, her family loved her, and she was just one of those people you just respected. She would be the doting grandmother when she grew old, totally dedicated to the litter of kids she would bear and all their descendants.

Over the years, life threw Marian a lot of curveballs. She remained solid in her faith and her commitment to her kids. But in February 2004, Marian couldn't finish a run because she was short of breath, a highly unusual experience for a woman who had completed three marathons and even a triathlon just months before. After she experienced continued difficulty breathing over the next few weeks, tests were eventually done and shortly after her fiftieth birthday the diagnosis was confirmed. Marian McBride Stevens, non-smoker, non-drinker, marathon runner, triathlon competitor, devout Catholic, devoted wife, and loving mother of five, had lung cancer.

The cancer had already metastasized into her chest wall and some neighboring organs. Chemo and radiation might prolong the inevitable but it would be a painful cost. We brought her home from the hospital to do home hospice and three months later she was taken to what hopefully is a better place. Visions of holding her in my arms as she took her final breaths while I watched the tears fall freely from two of her teenage children at the foot of the bed are constant reminders of the pain endured by kids who lose a parent too young.

If there is a God, there certainly is a special place in heaven for a mother of five children. Like her dad, she didn't get to enjoy the third trimester of her life. But unlike so many who are complicit in their demise, her premature death just left us all shaking our heads and hearts asking, "Why?"

This millennium has not been good to our family in terms of death. Maybe it was the sudden loss of my wife of twenty-seven years that moved me to write this book. Or the death of a good friend George Maly, who died of a neuromuscular disease. Or the death of my cousin Roger Corke to Parkinson's Disease, and his wife Joan, suddenly, a couple of years later leaving behind two beautiful daughters, Jenny and Susie, who have grown to become amazing young women. Or the death of my friend Buddy Venne, star hoop player at Holy Cross, high school teammates Jimmy Van Story and Jim Portray. Or the death of Steve Fink, father of one of my daughter Riley's best friends. Or the death of Gretchen Nowell, one of my daughter's other best friends' mom. Or the death of my sister-in-law, JoAnne Carlson, to pancreatic cancer two years ago. Or the death of one of my best friends, Gary "The Knute" Knutson, to colon cancer in 2005.

Those deaths had all haunted me, as did the tragic loss of several young people in our town who were close to my kids. We had at least five teen suicides in our town in four years, plus the tragic loss of one of my son, Casey's, best friends and teammates in a one-car accident a few blocks from our home. The suicide of another teammate came a short time later. Both of the kids' grandmothers died from lung cancer. Most recently we grappled with the suicide of one of Conor's best friends three days before Conor deployed to Iraq with the Marines. There was also the heartbreaking sudden death of a beautiful two-year-old girl Riley babysat for and adored.

So much death surrounded our family in so little time; the tragedy of it all numbed my senses. Too many funerals, too many tragic losses, too many tombstones of many of those losses only steps away from Marian's grave at Woodlawn Cemetery.

Most probably, though, it was Marian's death as well as that of one of my brothers six months before Marian's passing and the other six months after she passed away to a genetic neuromuscular disease called "Huntington's" which made me take up the pen. I'm not sure – maybe it was a combination of all of these unfortunate losses. But when I opened my e-mail in January 2008 and read about a college classmate and the disease he was battling, I didn't hesitate to hit the reply button.

So, this is not a story about my scrapbook or my family. I will comment on a few things about them, and someday I may write about that often incredibly painful journey, but not today.

This book is about the true story of an amazing man who will not be able to enjoy the fruits of his labor in life either. He did so much good for so many in the first fifty years on this planet. But what he has done in the last twenty-four months will ensure his legacy will be one that will inspire those of us who will love him forever – and maybe you, too.

He is in the latter stages of the battle of his life, and it is one he will lose, no matter how brave he is.

This is a story about courage, tragedy, perseverance, and faith.

This is the story of my friend Jimmy Culveyhouse, from Salem, Oregon.

Jimmy

Jimmy is an athlete, businessman, teacher, humanitarian, cancer survivor, Hepatitis C survivor, fundraiser, devoted husband, uncle, and one of the greatest salesmen I have ever met. He also is a character – mischievous, hard partier, and a guy who has lived life to the fullest. He sure did in the first two phases of his life.

In his first fifty years on this earth, Jimmy Culveyhouse's resume looks like a combination of *Rudy* and *Forest Gump* as he accomplished things most people only dream of doing:

- Little league all-star in baseball
- Star player on US Midwest champion biddy basketball team winning title and earning trip to World finals in Puerto Rico
- At age twelve, saluted with a parade in his & the team's honor in Merrillville, Indiana with a billboard put up proclaiming : "Merrillville, Home of Jim Culveyhouse", heady stuff for a twelve year old
- Earned nine letters in golf, tennis, and basketball in high school
- Member of the Andrean High School Hall of Fame in two sports, tennis and golf
- Won three Gary Metro doubles tennis titles, one singles regional title (including an upset of the number one seed "Juniors" player in the state)

- Started caddying at age ten and worked his way up to caddy master in Gary, Indiana
- Had one choice as to where to go to college, the University of Notre Dame
- Applied three times; was rejected three times
- After appealing before the whole admission board, in person with his high school Counselor, John Coggins, was finally accepted on probation; had to maintain a "B" average or he was out
- Paid for one hundred percent of his education by working two jobs in the summer, and three jobs while attending school and maintaining a "B" average; the jobs included: tarring basements, caddying, tending bar, and working as a night-shift fork lift operator
- At only five-foot-six, "walked on" to the Notre Dame golf team and earned four letters in varsity golf
- Set and still holds the course record (sixty-four) at Notre Dame's golf course
- Set and still holds the tournament record for seventy-two holes (274, eighteen below par) at the Burke Memorial Golf Course
- Member of the Monogram Club with his moniker permanently etched on the "Ring of Fame" in the Joyce Center, along with names like Hornung, Montana, Rockne, Austin Carr, and 2008 Basketball Hall of Fame inductee, his classmate, Adrian Dantley
- While there, ND won national championship in football
- Was there when the basketball team ended UCLA's basketball eighty-eight–game winning streak totaling the most season wins in ND history (twenty-six) and finished ranked number three
- Majored in business and wrote a marketing course thesis about fabled wine maker Ernest Gallo, of Gallo Wines, not knowing the professor knew him

- Was personally called in the bar where he worked, Corby's, while in college by Ernest Gallo himself with an offer to fly him out to Modesto, California, to visit the winery
- Given private tour, dined with all the Gallo family members, and offered job when he finished at Notre Dame
- Graduated from Notre Dame in 1976 with honors; a few days later started with Gallo Wines, working in Los Angeles
- Established numerous new initiatives in sales and merchandising, precedents for how Gallo still does business today in Southern California
- Promoted to positions of increased responsibilities by also helping put Gallo wines on the map in the restaurant industry by making Gallo "the house pour" in scores of top restaurants in Colorado
- Introduced Gallo products in Trinidad and most Caribbean countries where Gallo products are still well-established today
- Recruited by Coca-Cola and hired as marketing manager in the headquarters in Atlanta before eventually becoming director of sales, overseeing operations for sixteen Coca-Cola Bottling Co. plants in the NW
- Left Coke to start his own direct marketing company, which he ran successfully for five years before selling it
- With his wife, Melanie, opened Chuckles Gift shop in Salem, Oregon, expanding to three stores before selling the business
- Recognized by the Small Business Administration as runner-up winner in the state of Oregon as "small business of the year" and "small businessman of the year"
- Left the business world to become faculty member of Chemeketa Community College, taking over a floundering course for small businesses and transforming

it into one of the best small business outreach programs in America

- Helped more than six hundred companies in the Willamette Valley region
- While teaching, volunteered and served as chairperson for charities and organizations such as the March of Dimes, United Methodist Retirement Association, The McNary Real Estate Association, and was also a founding member and past president of the Creekside Golf course in Salem
- McNary Club Champion and Creekside Club Champion
- Has won other several golf awards and championships throughout the U.S.
- On October 4th, 2008 the Men's Golf Association and his club, Creekside Golf Club in Salem, Oregon initiated the "Jim Culveyhouse Award" that will be presented every year to the person that comes close to the standards that Jim has set. The inscription reads 2008 – Jim Culveyhouse Award – "In the Spirit of the Game": Presented to Jim Culveyhouse; In Selfless Service in Promoting the Game of Golf and in Support of our Creekside Golf Club. Given this day - October 4, 2008 by the MGA Membership
- Shot seventy-six at the Old Course at St. Andrews, Scotland, and seventy-five at Carnoustie Golf Club in Scotland, both courses renowned hosts of the British Open
- In addition: once dated a future Miss Universe; caddied for Arnold Palmer; sang and danced on stage with a senior Coke executive with Lionel Ritchie and the Commodores; dined with great actor Walter Matthau and heavyweight boxing champ Evander Holyfield; partied with Jack Nicholson, personal audiences with scores of other celebrities and politicians, the list is too long to include.

You get the idea. This is only a fraction of what Jimmy has accomplished in his life.

To be sure, the first fifty years of Jimmy Culveyhouse's life were filled with amazing accomplishments and a lot of very funny stories. It was not so much what he did, but how he did it that makes him someone you should get to know. His creativity, his energy, his organizational skills, his perseverance and his passion have been infectious to all. He probably could have continued up the corporate ladder and earned millions, but the call to serve those in his community became too strong to go unanswered.

Jimmy doesn't have any kids of his own. He and his wife Melanie celebrated their twenty-sixth wedding anniversary on March 26, 2009. There probably will not be a twenty-seven-year celebration because Jimmy is dying from a disease that ignores his accomplishments, the wishes of his friends and family. Its mission is singular in purpose: to kill my friend, Jimmy Culveyhouse.

After I hit the reply button to an e-mail Professor John Gasky sent in January alerting many about Jim's disease, this book began – not the story, but the book. Folks, I am not a writer. I am an ex-jock, businessman, father of five, and a frustrated actor. But after reconnecting with Jim and hearing his story, he asked me if I would write this book. There are many people on this planet I can say no to. Jimmy Culveyhouse is not one of them. So, please do not focus on my primitive writing skills. It is Jim's life that counts here, and how he is trying to help others. His legacy will be one in which his wife, recently adopted daughters, Pari and Sarah, his friends, and all of his family will take great pride.

The Disease

Lou Gehrig's disease is what it is commonly referred to by the majority of us common folk who are devoid of medical training. Also broadly referred to in its abbreviated acronym form, it is an insidious disease that strikes without warning or forbearing.

It is inoperable and incurable, and if ever a disease were deserving of this description, it is just down right inhumane.

Amyotrophic Lateral Sclerosis. You may have never heard of it. You may not be able to even pronounce it. But if someone you know or love ever develops it, you will never forget it. To those that have the disease, the most despicable letters in the English language aren't IRS or KKK. They are, unquestionably, ALS.

As quoted from the home website for ALS: "Amyotrophic lateral sclerosis (ALS) is a progressive neuromuscular disease that weakens and eventually destroys motor neurons (components of the nervous system that connect the brain with the skeletal muscles). Skeletal muscles are involved with voluntary movements, such as walking and talking. The motor neurons transmit the command to move from the brain to the skeletal muscles, which respond by contracting."

The website continues: "A person with ALS usually presents with problems in dexterity or gait resulting from muscle weakness, or with difficulty speaking or swallowing. Sphincter control, sensory function, intellectual ability, and skin integrity are preserved. Patients become paralyzed and often require ventilation and surgery to provide a new opening in the stomach (gastrostomy). Loss of respiratory function is ultimately the cause of death."

So, bottom line, ALS is a disease contrived by a would-be devil.

Let's think of some of the worst things we can do to someone, medically. I know – let's take away their ability to function, to be able to take care of themselves, to breathe, and to be able to clean themselves after defecating. But let's leave them with total mental and intellectual functions. Let's also make sure we keep all of their sensory abilities in place so they can feel all the pain and embarrassment which accompanies this illness.

Ah, that's good, that's good, the Devil must think, *but what else?*

Let's make sure they can't swallow properly so doctors have to drill a hole in their chest walls and insert a tube for feeding. Oh, and by the way, you forgot something. Let's make the disease progressive. Have it start from the legs and let it work its way up to the lungs. Or, let's offer an alternative – start at the top, and let's mess up the person's speech so badly that people think they are drunk at lunchtime when they haven't even touched a cocktail. From there let's take the north/south route to the lungs. If the disease has two major ways of manifesting, we can really catch them by surprise and fool them into thinking it might be something less severe.

ALS must be a demonic creation; there is no other explanation.

ALS was first categorized as a disease back in 1869. There are three known types of ALS. In 1993, it was discovered that about fifteen percent of the cases are related to a hereditary mutation. That type of ALS is what they call "familial."

The other eighty-five percent of cases cannot be linked at this time to anything genetic or environmental. But there are two elements of the unknown ALS cases. About eighty-five percent of the remaining cases are what is called "limb-onset" ALS. That means the disease starts in the limbs – the arms and legs – and then takes the long route to its ultimate destination, the lungs. Lou Gehrig died from this type of ALS.

The remaining fifteen percent of ALS cases are classified as "bulbar." In this instance, the disease starts in the head and first manifests itself in slurred speech. Other symptoms ensue with the final target again being the lungs. With a shorter route to the lungs from the head than from the limbs, those with Bulbar ALS usually have the shortest life expectancy.

Jimmy has Bulbar ALS.

According to the Center for ALS, at any time, there are an estimated thirty thousand people in the United States with ALS. You may not consider that as very much since we are a people of over three hundred million. But the simple fact is that the average life expectancy of a person who develops ALS after diagnosis is only three to five years. They don't stay around long enough to build up the statistical significance associated with more widely known maladies.

Various forms of cancer kill many more people annually and we rightfully celebrate when a cancer patient goes "into remission." ALS patients do not go into remission. They have received a death sentence for which there is no commutation.

Bobby Knight, the famed former college basketball coach, once proclaimed: "Everyone has the will to win, but few have the will to prepare to win." The same might be said about life. But once diagnosed with ALS, no matter how strong the patient's will to live is, one must make a fundamental decision: how will you choose to live the rest of your abbreviated life?

I knew Jim more than thirty years ago when I was a student at the University of Notre Dame. He was two years younger than me and I knew him basically as the diminutive bartender at my favorite hang-out, Corby's Tavern, in South Bend, Indiana. Because of his size, someone gave him the nickname "Stump."

Nicknames were big at Notre Dame. Many of us played for "Digger." I was "Hawk." The rest of the gang of jocks I hung with included "Geek," "Goose," "Zat," "Loz," "Duke," "Big T," "Ghost," and the aforementioned Dr. Gasky when he was a student on what appeared to be the ten-year plan. Well, he was and always will be simply "Gasman." Again, you get the idea. In fact, I didn't even know Jimmy Culveyhouse's real name – he was just "Stump."

Regretfully, I didn't really know him or spend much time trying to back then. I was a BMOC ("big man on campus"), or so I was told (OK, so I thought). As a varsity basketball player on a nationally ranked team and vice president of the Senior Class of '74, with a campus radio show to boot, I was fairly well known, although sometimes not for the reasons I intended. But, irrespective of what he did or who he was as a person, when I showed up at Corby's with my posse, he was only "Stump" to me, the generous provider of a constant flow of free beer for my friends and me. Regardless of his physical stature, Stump was more important to many in this watering hole than any BMOC. He was a BMAC – big man at Corby's.

I remember Stump as always a guy with a smile on his face. "Stump, another round for the boys!" *Smile.* "Stump, how about some pretzels?" *Smile.* "Stump, change the channel." *Smile.*

In hindsight, he was like the farm boy, Westley, in one of my favorite movies of all time, *The Princess Bride.* Whenever Buttercup asks her farm boy Westley for something, he responds, "As you wish." At Corby's, when the boys ordered something, Jimmy's smile quietly responded, "As you wish." But Stump's verbal response would be a bit different and it would become his calling card for life. He would always respond, "No problem."

I had no idea at the time what road he traveled to get to Notre Dame nor did I have any idea he was any kind of athlete. I never bothered to ask. I was too busy being "the Hawk," a persona which allowed me to be known by many. I was on stage so much that I had little time to let anyone get close to me. Jock, campus celeb, class clown, character impersonator, class VP, I was "on" all the time and I certainly spent little time getting to know an undersized underclassman with a lousy mustache. Of course, Stump did not know that. As long as the free beers flowed I could make anyone seem like my best friend.

So, the truth is, this is not a story about an old friend from college. It is a story about an acquaintance from Notre Dame. But I can proudly say now, it is a story about a man I admire as much as anyone I have ever known. So it's really a story about a new friend.

I am not a BMOC anymore, not even in my own mind. Stump has become a bigger man than I could ever hope to be. Unlike *The Princess Bride* or Ozzie and Harriet, Stump's life is not a fantasy. I wish I had taken the time to get to know him thirty years ago because I might have been able to enjoy much of his wonderful ride. If I hadn't been so absorbed in my own world, I know he and I would have become close, as close as we are now, thirty years later.

As I write this, it has only been a year since we reconnected, but there is a bond now that is one of which I am very proud, and I don't want it to end. I want our friendship to last, to be one of those "miracles on ice." "*Do you believe in miracles?*" Great call, Al

Michaels. C'mon God, it's been twenty-eight years since that miracle. This is a good man. If you can do that for a hockey team, you can do this for a guy many of us wish we could emulate.

The trouble is that Stump has ALS. He doesn't have much time left on this earth. He never saw it coming. And while, unmistakably, when he learned of his fate, it shook him, he quickly determined that for whatever time he had left on this earth, he would take his will to live, his will to win, and do everything he could to help find a cure for ALS.

After you get to know Stump, you will understand that if there were a Hall of Fame for over-achievers, this man would be a first ballot entry. His early life reads like a combination of *Rudy*, *Forrest Gump*, and *Rocky* rolled into one.

Since being diagnosed with ALS, his courage is similar to that of Professor Morrie Schwartz, about whom Mitch Albom so eloquently wrote in *Tuesdays With Morrie*. It also mirrors much of Bruce Edwards' life and story. Bruce was the long-time caddie and friend of famed PGA tour golfer Tom Watson. Bruce's story was chronicled so ably by the prolific author John Feinstein in *Caddie for Life*. If you haven't read either book, you should. Both compassionately portray the journeys of two very special people whose lives were cut short by ALS.

Josh Billings, a major league catcher in the early twentieth century said: "The key to happiness in life is not in holding good cards, but in playing well those you are dealt." Stump, like Lou Gehrig, Morrie, and Bruce, was dealt aces and eights, the dead man's hand. But wow, has he played the cards he has been dealt well.

While I have some vices, gambling is not one of them. My statistics teacher at Notre Dame, Professor Curme, taught me about a thing called "odds." He used to go to Las Vegas regularly, and with all due respect to the good teacher, no one would mistake him for George Clooney. That probably actually played to his benefit because he was a statistical wizard and he kind of flew below the radar screen. In those days, Professor Curme used to do well in Vegas. He knew the odds on just about everything. My guess is he could count cards with the best of them and he had a system of wagering not based on gut, but on good old statistics. Stats have never been my strong suit. I aced his class during the summer of '72, more probably because I was a jock. It certainly wasn't for my statistical or intuitive skills. In Vegas, luck is for suckers. Playing the odds right is what winners do.

But sometimes, no matter how lucky you think you are, you can't beat the odds. You have a better chance of hitting the lottery in most states or striking it rich in Vegas than in developing ALS. Only one in about a hundred thousand people develop the disease. Those are pretty long odds and Vegas puts them up all the time. Morehead State, the sixty-four seed in this year's March Madness had better odds of beating the number-one-ranked Louisville Cardinals than someone developing ALS. But if that is the math, someone has to be the statistical anomaly, and James Kevin Culveyhouse, my friend we call Stump, is the unlucky one in this book. But Morehead State didn't beat the Cardinals this year and Stump won't beat ALS.

Both Morrie Schwartz and Bruce Edwards are gone from this earth. They left us just as "the Ironman," Lou Gehrig, did in 1941. You don't need to be a sports fan to remember Lou Gehrig. He was the backbone of the greatest baseball dynasty ever, the New York Yankees of the 1920s and 1930s. He hit 493 career homers, set a career record for grand slams with twenty-three, and after replacing Wally Pip at first base in 1925, he played in 2,130 consecutive games for the Yankees. It wasn't until the symptoms of fatigue and muscular coordination difficulty forced him to yield his position to Babe Dahlgren in 1939. It was a record which stood for decades until Cal Ripken Jr. broke it a few years ago.

Lou died of ALS. But the disease was not well known in those days. The flu epidemic of the second decade of the century had claimed millions of lives. Diseases like smallpox, tuberculosis, and cancer were far more common. But ultimately, after doctors could find no other possibility and as the Ironman's strength continued to wane, the diagnosis was made. It was a shock to American sports fans. For the younger generation, the reaction was not dissimilar to that when we heard when Earvin "Magic" Johnson announced he was HIV positive. But Magic admitted he had made errors in judgment which led to his demise. The Ironman, like everyone else who has developed ALS, did nothing other than be "the one."

If you are a movie buff as old as I am, you have probably seen and cried at *The Pride of the Yankees* when near the end of the movie, Gary Cooper, as Lou, steps to the microphone in Yankee Stadium in 1939 and utters those famous words which still echo through the runways of the "house that Ruth built:" "Today, I consider myself the luckiest man on the face of the earth." Less than two years later, at the age of only thirty-eight, Lou Gehrig died. This July 4, 2009, marks the seventieth anniversary of that speech.

This was a man who, with all due respect to the Babe, may have been the most feared hitter in the game. He had a lot more baseball to play but had to give up the game he loved because of those three words: amyotrophic lateral sclerosis.

Not many had ever heard of this disease before they learned of Gehrig's diagnosis. It was hard to pronounce and so unfamiliar to the public that they needed something more easily identifiable to refer to it in order to discuss this tragedy. So they simply started referring to this quiet killer as "Lou Gehrig's Disease."

Since he learned he had ALS, Jimmy has exhibited a fierce determination to try to raise money for research. As I write these words, Stump is still with us, battling to stay alive to raise awareness and money to help find a cure so that maybe someday others may not have to go through this physiological torture.

For those who have ALS, if there is a "hell on earth," it surely lies in the bowels of this disease.

Shortly after he turned fifty, Jimmy was diagnosed with and beat prostate cancer. That was almost immediately followed by an almost fatal bout with Hepatitis C, a nasty strain for which there is only about a two percent survival rate. The grim reaper had thrown two of his best shots at my friend. Maybe the reaper was upset because, like he had done so many times in his life, Stump had beaten the odds again and again. He had overcome so much in his life and then he beat cancer and Hepatitis C. I guess that is one way to look at it.

I prefer an alternate possibility. The devil may have developed the disease, but God is bringing Jimmy home. Just like Christ had to suffer so much on the cross and in the beatings preceding His death, God is trying to teach us all a lesson through Jimmy – probably many lessons, such as the need to realize that this journey of life should not be take for granted. Or that through Jim's suffering, we can all stop for a while and stop being so selfish and do something nice for those less fortunate: to not look the other way when we see someone hurting or in need, but to stop and do something about it.

Jimmy's mantra is, "Whatever you give to someone, you receive back twice in return."

Through Jim's life we can learn that, as someone once said, "It is not the size of the dog in the fight but rather the fight in the dog," and "When the going gets tough, the tough get going."

His dad taught him that trait; he taught Jimmy a lot of things. But Jimmy's childhood, while filled with many accomplishments in which he could take justifiable pride, was also filled with a lot of pain. And through the pain came learning, with a steadfast commitment that the painful lessons he learned from his dad were not ones he would ever impart to children, if he ever had them.

Jimmy's Childhood

Born less than a hundred miles to the west of South Bend, young Jim was, for the first eighteen years of his life, an only child to Jim and Rita Culveyhouse. Being an only child was a mixed blessing. He received all the attention from his parents, both good and bad. Jim's recollection of his childhood is painful as he recalls it today. Recent e-mails from his dad reveal a hardness that still hurts his gravely ill adult son. The following recollections are Jim's and he has approved of what has been written about his mom and dad.

A salesman for Monroe Calculators in Chicago Heights, James Culveyhouse Sr. was a gregarious man, one who commanded the stage wherever he went. While this trait served him well in his early years at Monroe, upon arriving home for dinner, in the eyes of his son, it manifested itself in a controlling, surly demeanor whose sole mission seemed to be the unhappiness and sadness of his wife and his under-sized son. Alcohol was his frequent companion. While America may "run on Dunkin'" today, Jimmy recalls, after work, his dad ran on booze.

James Sr. suffered his own tragedy as a child when his father disappeared from his life at the age of nine. According to Jimmy, he just left and never came back. Maybe it was a damaged inner child or his incomplete relationship with his father which fueled his anger and insecurity, but his insensitivity to the feelings of his small family was so pronounced, as Stump recalls, it seemed to border on psychotic.

Always the opportunist, James fell in love with the daughter of the an executive of US Steel, Rita Louise Quinlan. She was a petite sweet girl and she was swept away by the muscular blue-collar kid from the other side of Gary. After a brief courtship, they married on May 16, 1953.

The American automotive industry was in its heyday. Names such as Toyota, Nissan, and Honda weren't a part of the American lexicon in the 1950s. General Motors and Ford, along with their Detroit cousins, Chrysler and American Motors, dominated the automotive market, the airwaves, and the aspirations of Midwesterners. The demand for US Steel was epic and one of the leading producers of the gleaming iron derivative was good old Gary, Indiana.

Gary is situated on the southern shores of Lake Michigan, tucked away in the northwest corner of the Hoosier state. Its most famous thoroughfare is I-90, the Chicago Skyway. With the oceanic-like Lake Michigan easily able to accommodate the daily traffic of barges, Gary residents and factories would crank out the steel right next to the lake. Rather than opt for the more expeditious, yet expensive, overland route to Detroit, steel-toting ships the length of football fields would transport Gary's finest north across the open waters of Lake Michigan and wave at Traverse City, before doing the "big bend."

After negotiating the turbulent waters of Lake Michigan, barges would then squeeze through the passage just below the "U.P." en route to the more shallow and friendlier Lake Huron. Then it was downhill from there. Hugging the eastern shore of the automotive state, freighters would ease around "the thumb." Then, after squeezing through the canal that separates Michigan from Windsor Ontario, they would settle into eastern ports closer to their cherished product's final destination, any one of scores of assembly plants. Gary produced steel for a lot of industries but was codependent on the health of Detroit and proud of it.

To grow up in Gary or to work in any of its fabled factories meant you had to be tough. And even if you weren't tough, you sure better know how to act like it. The elder Culveyhouse had survived growing up in Gary. In fact, he conquered one of the town's cherished prizes in young Rita, daughter of the an executive of the largest steel mill east of Pittsburgh.

Shortly after James and Rita were married, the good Lord blessed them with a son on January 13, 1954. Not surprisingly, they chose to name him James. But he was not to be a James Jr., the son of James Robert Culveyhouse. No one was worthy of that mantle. The boy would have to be his own man, James Kevin Culveyhouse.

From the outset, little Jimmy was more raised by his doting mother, with cameo appearances from his father. In the 1950s, a woman's place was at home. But Rita loved to teach. After young Jim reached the age where he would enroll in school, Rita took up a job as a third grade teacher in the local public elementary school. Rita would get Jimmy up and drive him to school ensuring that he always represented the Culveyhouse family with pride: shoes polished, shirt and pants pressed, hair combed, and a smile on his face.

When Jimmy was nine, the family escaped the sooty skylines of Gary and set up shop in Merrillville, Indiana. Rita missed Gary in many ways, but life would be great in Merrillville.

After tending to the demands of precocious third graders, Rita would rush to pick up Jimmy from school and then chauffeur him to any number of activities in which he would be involved. With each birthday, Jimmy seemed to not just advance in years and grade, but in his athletic prowess as well. Whether it was as a nine-year-old star shortstop on the Junedale Little League All Star Team, or as the playmaker on the Merrillville biddy basketball team, Jim sought out and found the feeling of family in sports.

Whether from his coaches who inspired him, or from teammates who encouraged him, Jim felt at home in the arena of sports. It was on the hardwood where Jim would get his first taste of stardom. But he never would have taken up basketball had it not been for the encouragement of his mom.

Jim recalls when his mom brought him to the basketball try-outs for "biddy basketball." He was afraid – of new kids, of being too small, of failure. He refused to get out of the car. But his gentle mom was persistent. She knew it was fear holding him back and she used her finest teacher's instincts to inspire her timid son to open the car door to a new opportunity. She used words to the effect of, "Jimmy, just go in there and have fun and do your best. That is all you can do. The other kids are probably more anxious than you are. Just go in and have fun."

With that, Jimmy took the chance, and as fate would have it, he fell in love with basketball and basketball fell in love with Jimmy. Jim remembers it was his mom who always seemed to be there for him when he was a child. He bemoans the fact that his father never saw him play. Memories like that create scars in a boy and a lot of pain. It is what you do with that pain that defines a life.

It wasn't Jim's dad who was so instrumental in his participation in sports. Five days a week, the elder James would leave the house early, work hard selling adding machines and fancy new calculators, before often knocking off work to enjoy a few libations with the boys before heading down the Calumet Expressway toward home. As Jimmy remembers, James' interest in his son's activities was rarely in evidence. While some fathers of only sons would dote on and push hard for their sons to become the next Mickey Mantle, Paul Hornung, or Bob Cousy, young Jim remembers his father seemed to more interested in what young Jim did wrong, than what he did right.

Even the nickname the elder Culveyhouse chose for his son, one which he would still address him by in his later years, did not evoke feelings of affection or aspiration. Kids who were called by their dads "Sport," "Buddy," "Son," or – God forbid – "Junior," could wear those labels with pride and it was music to their ears to hear their dads call them out. But it's hard to feel a lot of pride when your father continually refers to you as "Toad."

After teaching all day, Rita would taxi Jimmy to and from practices and then get home and get to work. Somehow each night, by the time Dad arrived home, the house was spotless and a hot meal was ready for all. Both Rita and Jimmy eagerly awaited the man from whom all they wanted was affection and approval. Rita tried to always do something special in the preparation of dinner, but it was rarely acknowledged. It just came to be expected.

As the years progressed, the timeliness of his dad's arrivals at home each night became less reliable. His interest in and affection for young Jimmy continued to dissipate. What did not wane was his surly demeanor, displayed continually to a despondent wife and an increasingly disappointed boy. The words that echo in his ears weren't "I am proud of you" but rather, "You could have done better."

Seemingly angry at God for delivering to him an under-sized offspring, his expectations for greatness could never be met. It had to be his wife's fault. Or maybe it was the scrawny little kid, a poor excuse for a Culveyhouse son, who was to blame. Either way, over the years of his youth, neither Jimmy nor his mom could assuage the anger of the family bully. To the outside world he was good old fun-lovin' Jim. To his young son, he was the reincarnation of Ebenezer Scrooge.

Jimmy was usually the smallest kid in his class. It was a distinction that would be a burden to him through the early years amidst his merciless peers. But as the "Toad" aged, he overcame his stature by acquiring skills in sports indifferent to size. By the time his parents enrolled him in St. Mark's Catholic School, a leg of lamb weighed more than young Jim. This was a boy who would probably get carded until he was at least thirty.

Certain that he was raising a "momma's boy," the elder Culveyhouse showed less interest in his bubbly son than he did the sports page of the *Chicago Tribune,* and certainly not as much as his dear Canadian Club. Yes, Jimmy was indeed his mother's son, for it was lovely Rita who taught him, inspired him, nurtured him, and encouraged him – his mom as well as her mother, Jimmy's beloved Nana, Helen Quinlan.

Widowed in her mid-forties when her successful but hard-driving spouse collapsed of a heart attack not long after Jimmy was born, Nana deflected her grief by spending time with her young grandson. In fact, in order to give her daughter a night out each week, she insisted on bringing young Jim to her well-appointed home. When Jimmy came to visit, it was a mutual admiration society with a population of two.

If you asked most kids in school what their least favorite day of the week was, the vast majority would most likely select Monday, back to school day. However, in his early childhood, Jimmy recalls the day of the week he dreaded most was not Monday, but Friday, and his favorite day of the week was, not surprisingly, Saturday, but not for reasons most would expect.

Every Friday seemed to be a "Black Friday" for young Jim as that was the day his dad, weary of the affairs of the week, would come home to enjoy his extra ration of libations. With the augmented consumption came an increased flow of insults. Little that Jimmy might have achieved during the week was enough to satisfy his brow-beating father. If he was quiet, he was criticized. If he talked out of turn, he was criticized. And if he talked back, well, he was more than just criticized.

Conversely, after learning how to survive the Friday night fights, Jim could not wait for Saturday. The evening of the seventh day of the week was Nana's gift to her daughter. She would insist on having Jimmy come to her home for a sleepover, allowing Rita to enjoy some adult time with James. Most of the time, Rita and her husband would enjoy a night of playing bridge at a neighbor's house. Jimmy really didn't care. He wished every night was Saturday night.

Jimmy recalled his Nana as a meticulous lady who had more class than any woman he ever knew. Her beautiful home featured lovely antiques, big chairs and beds that seemed to swallow you up in an orgasm of comfort. Nana had her routines and she had a wonderful way of making Jimmy feel special.

One of the rituals Jimmy could always rely on was the trip to the corner pharmacy. There, Nana would allocate to the youngster a couple of nickels and allow him free choice to pick the treat of this preference. To this day, Jim recalls this wonderful gesture as something his wise grandmother knew would put a smile on his face, no matter how trying the events of the past several days may have been.

Jimmy recalls with great fondness the mother figures in his life. While the memories of his father are not what he wished he could recall, he acknowledges that right or wrong, his father remained faithful to his mother and to the surprise package that was delivered to Rita some eighteen years after Jimmy was born.

Maybe it was in celebration of Jimmy going off to college, but on at least one occasion when they least expected, their infrequent moments of intimacy ended up with a wonderful blessing. A beautiful daughter, Shawn Culveyhouse, was born to Jim and Rita during Jimmy's freshman year at Notre Dame.

In Boston, this was what the locals would call a "wicked shocka'." Maybe because Shawn was a girl or maybe the elder Culveyhouse had learned from his mistakes with his parenting of Jimmy, but the relationship Shawn would enjoy with Big Jim was far more congenial than that which he experienced with Jimmy.

With the age difference, Jimmy and Shawn were not close growing up. He really became more like an uncle than a big brother. Jimmy would graduate from Notre Dame and be off to make his mark with his first job before Shawn would even enter the first grade. While he always remembered his sister with cards and gifts at the appropriate time, the awkwardness he felt in the relationship with his dad demanded he avoid coming home except for the requisite holiday visits.

It would not be until much later in life that Jim and Shawn would enjoy the kind of brother/sister relationship both coveted.

When Nana died, something inside of Jimmy went with her too. Always remembering her for her tenderness and kindness toward him, Jimmy privately grieved a long time after Nana passed away. When he would come home, he would often head to Gary to her home and just sit trying to savor each fond memory of Saturday nights there.

But the impact of Nana's death was not just felt by Jimmy. It devastated his mom, Rita. With Nana gone, Rita's desire to "keep it all together" seemed to vanish – almost overnight, as Jimmy recalls.

While Nana's passing was not unexpected, Rita just seemed to quit on things that used to be important to her. Rita had always enjoyed keeping her husband company by drinking with him. But after

Nana died, both the quantity consumed and the frequency of the consumption increased. The expression "drowned her sorrows in the bottom of a bottle" seemed to apply fittingly, recalls Jimmy.

Jimmy tried to help his mom get sober, but any insinuation that Rita had a drinking problem was met with the full fury of her enabling husband. She was just sad and deserved the right to drown her sorrows screamed the actions or rather inactions of the elder Culveyhouse. Since Jim Sr. had lost his job at Monroe, his motivation for life also seemed to evaporate. So there they would be each day, just sitting and waiting for the sun to go down so they could enjoy their cocktails exactly at 5:00 p.m.

As Jimmy reflects on his youth there is a profound sadness as he describes the frustration with being a lonely boy who only wanted the approval of his father. He never got it when he was the star player on a biddy basketball team that shocked the biddy basketball world with a "Hoosiers-like" win in a national tournament in Puerto Rico. Big Jim could have watched the semi-final upset win led by Jimmy, but instead he chose a night out with the boys.

He never got his father's approval when the town where they lived at the time – Merrillville, Indiana – threw a parade and had posters with Jimmy's name on it celebrating not only the team's victory but Jimmy's selection on the tournament first team all-stars.

He never got it when he was a star player on a little league baseball all-star team when he batted .610.

He never got it winning any one of his nine letters at Andrean High School in tennis, baseball, and golf.

He never got it when the high school inducted Jimmy into its athletic Hall of Fame for both tennis and golf.

And he never got it despite all the accomplishments in college or in the academic world. Jimmy feels as if he has tried to reach out to his father so many times to try to establish a father/son connection he has always desired. Jimmy will take to his grave many regrets but none more painful than the lifelong rejection of his father.

Stump also regrets that of all the habits or behavior he would adopt from his father, hard drinking was the biggest.

From college throughout his professional careers, Jimmy has always enjoyed his cocktails, beer and wine mostly. But while his partying ways produced some very funny stories, it always produced some painful moments as well. As he reflects on them, he can still laugh at the good times, but he also knows his drinking cost him a lot in his career.

Fortunately, while his father to this day still seems to ignore the sorry state Jimmy's mom is in due to excessive drinking, Jimmy finally answered the wake-up call. As his life progressed, Jimmy learned to dial it back and enjoy alcohol as intended – in moderation.

It's often said that the pain that doesn't kill you will make you stronger. As I listen to Jimmy's recollection of his youth, I am struck by the similarities of our experiences. Alcoholic fathers, the feeling of emotional abandonment, the escape of the pain through sports, trying to always please everyone by making them laugh, over-achieving to prove how great you are, and yes, too much drinking.

If Jimmy and I were kids together, we would have undoubtedly been running mates. And God, it would have been fun.

Notre Dame

Growing up about an hour from Notre Dame, the dream of attending the school became an obsession to Jimmy. He learned early on to set his sights high and develop a plan to achieve them.

Les Brown said, "Shoot for the moon. Even if you miss it, you will land among the stars." That typifies how Jimmy doggedly pursued his goal of attending Notre Dame.

At Andrean High School, Jimmy took courses he really didn't want to take. His teachers were polite, almost patronizing, with several of them maintaining attitudes like, "Yes, you can get into Notre Dame." Their words said yes, but their body language most often said, "Yeah, sure."

But he did have some people at Andrean, such as John Coggins, who believed in him. They compensated for the lack of support from his dad and provided the fuel to help keep his dream alive.

In addition to making the honor roll in class, Jimmy played sports year round. In the fall, it was tennis. In the winter months, he was a feisty point guard who would not back down from any challenges. And in the spring, it was back outside to play baseball, tennis, and golf.

Jimmy kept telling all of his friends he was going to go to Notre Dame. Most of them just laughed too.

His dream of going to Notre Dame reminds me of the story I heard about the great country music star, Dolly Parton. At her small high school each student would announce what they would do with their lives. Responses of "I'm going to be a teacher" or "I'm going to be a doctor" or "I'm going to college" were invariably met with applause.

When Dolly blurted out, "I'm going to be a country music star," a cacophony of laughter and jeers filled the room. Dolly recalls that it was at that moment she knew nothing or no one was going to stand in her way. She would make them eat their words and by golly she did just that.

Jimmy developed the same type of resolve. He took his SAT and ACT college boards and did, well, OK. But with his good grades, athletic accomplishments, and his resume of working hard to save money, Jimmy was confident he would get in.

Jimmy had the grades, the scores, and the accomplishments to get into just about any school and he was recruited for potential full scholarships to several schools for golf.

But Jimmy's mission was sole in its purpose: attend Notre Dame, even if he had to pay for it himself.

Jimmy applied to Notre Dame. Jimmy was rejected.

Jimmy applied again to Notre Dame. Jimmy was rejected

Hoping the third time was a charm, undeterred, Jimmy applied again.

And for the third time, Jimmy was rejected.

Now most people that I know would have probably stopped, certainly after the second rejection. I don't know many who would have even had the nerve to apply a third time.

But to Jimmy, "No" doesn't mean "No, you can't." "No" means "No, you haven't given me enough reasons why I should say yes."

Jimmy learned early on that "when the buyer says 'No' that's when the sale begins"!

So Jimmy altered his game plan. He enlisted the support of every family friend and relative he knew who would help him by writing a letter on behalf. John Coggins did so willingly.

His final chance would be the opportunity to actually appear before the Board of Admissions and state his case. It reminds me of the movie *The Shawshank Redemption*. When Morgan Freeman's character, Ray, goes before the parole board for the "umpteenth" time, and he thinks there is little chance, he finally scores.

And so did Jimmy Culverhouse. Told he would be let in on a probationary basis, Jimmy was to enter the class of 1972. He was to maintain a "B" average or the door would probably hit him on the way out.

Jimmy was going to be a freshman at the University of Notre Dame. Remember when Matt Damon's character in *Good Will Hunting* scored Minnie Driver's phone number over the efforts of other "Hahhhhvard" suitors in a Cambridge bar? I bet Jimmy greeted his hometown doubters with a Matt Damon-like boast of, "How do like them apples?"

Jimmy had worked hard all of his life to save money. He gives his dad credit for respecting and saving money, much of which financed his education. He also gives his parents credit for the Catholic school education they financed in his early years. But Notre Dame and the attendant bills would be his burden and his alone.

His parents had put him through private schools as a young boy at St. Mark's, St. Peter and Paul, and then footed the bill for this Andrean High School education. But Jimmy had been told by Big Jim that if he wanted to go to Notre Dame, he was on his own.

Always hard working, Jimmy had started caddying at Gary Country Club when he was ten years old. The initial infatuation with golf quickly blossomed into what would become a lifelong love affair.

Jimmy worked as a caddy virtually every weekend that the course was open. He would caddy all weekend and he learned the game from so many different perspectives, including what to do and what not to do, the importance of honesty and integrity, how to keep your cool under pressure, and how not to get down after a bad shot.

He also knew that he actually had an advantage in golf with a tighter swing path than taller people. Size doesn't always matter.

After several years of caddying, Jimmy became the caddy master. As a precocious teenager who had quickly developed a good game of his own, Jimmy learned how to be with and talk to adults in the language they understood. It would serve him well throughout life but never more so than when he appeared before the Board of Admissions at Notre Dame.

Once he entered the university it was his work ethic that took over. In his own words:

"In my freshman year, I was on probation the first year as I was one of the last people accepted, so I had to study hard while working two summer jobs while also playing on the golf team.

"In my sophomore year, I had to work even harder. After classes I worked another job while also playing on the golf team. There never seemed to be enough money or time, so in order to save on my partying money, I took up another job as a bartender at one of the hot college bars, Corby's.

"After I would close-up Corby's at 2:00 a.m., I then worked two hours as a short-order cook before I would head back to my room for a quick nap and then off to classes – and of course then the golf course for competition."

Attending Notre Dame, no matter how busy you were, there were always opportunities to give back to the community. The LaFortune Center invited students to volunteer helping out special needs children and adults. Despite his frantic schedule, Jimmy volunteered there.

One of his favorite professors, the dean of the business school, Vince Raymond, had a favorite children's center for disadvantaged kids, where Jimmy volunteered.

When the university sponsored a program to deliver groceries to needy families during Thanksgiving, Jimmy delivered groceries to needy families.

While many of his buddies took off to Florida for spring break, Jimmy headed to North Carolina to play golf but also each year visited and bunked with the service men and women in the Marines at Camp Le Jeune.

As Jimmy reflected on Notre Dame and what it meant to him, he mused:

"I have based my life on the Golden Rule: Do unto others as you would have them do unto you. Respecting everyone, regardless of their station in life; keeps you humble and aware of your blessings. The spirit, tradition, and reputation of Notre Dame are so long-standing and huge that being a 'BMOC' seemed improbable, if not impossible. No one person could compare to the University of Notre Dame. I was just honored to be there and be part of it.

"Be your own person, period. Always think of others and follow that wonderful 'Irish Spirit.' Write down your short- and long-term plans and how you are going to achieve them. Make sure your life is balanced and stay focused on your goals. Become a "to-do list" person. You get more done that way. God, family, work, and service to others should be cornerstones of your life. We all make our own decisions.

"Most importantly, whatever you give to others, I guarantee you will get twice in return."

Jimmy's philosophy on life reminds me of one of my favorite quotes from the great entertainer Jimmy Durante and it is dead on: "Be nice to the people you meet on the way up, 'cause you never know who you will run into on the way down."

One of the jobs Stump worked at while at Notre Dame was at a small neighborhood bar called Corby's. Located about a mile for the edge of the campus, Joe Corby's dark, dimly lit tavern was one of many local watering holes for Irish students. Rocco's, Nicky's, the Library – there were others, but none of them captured the affection of some of Notre Dame's more fabled partiers, bartenders and characters than Corby's: Benks, Duff, Brad, Gasman, Boots, Mac, his roommate and best ND buddy, and of course Stump.

Mike "Mac" McDonald was one of Jimmy's very best friends at Notre Dame. A catcher on the Irish baseball team, Mac was not only great friends with Jimmy, they were co-bartenders at Corby's. To say they were competitive was an understatement. Although their college sports were different, they loved to go at each other in everything else – cards, basketball, tennis, you name it. They even boxed against each other in the famous Bengal Bouts, a campus traditional boxing tournament. Three rounds of beating the heck out of each other in front of thousands, then a hug and a few beers together at Corby's.

Mac and Jimmy rented a house their senior year right next to Corby's. It was a short commute home after long nights of either bartending or belting a few down. They could have used an interior decorator. Their coffee table was a wooden door and their source of entertainment was one of the original style black-and-white Zeniths. With his academic course load, part-time jobs, and golf team demands, Jimmy didn't focus much on housekeeping.

At Corby's, Benks, Boots, Mac, and Stump would command the back bar during the hectic hours of the weekend, which invariably started Wednesday for the less dedicated students and student athletes. Always resplendently clad in bib overalls and a black Corby's tee shirt, Stump recalls with great fondness his nights tending bar at Corby's. He was more like an orchestra leader than a bartender. He always knew what you drank and upon entering, he would usually hand you your first before you ever even asked for it.

Stump tells the story about one patron, John Prendergass. Of all Jimmy's "usual customers," Prendergass spent more money than anyone. While many of us only dreamed of more free rounds, Prendergass was always willing to pay for his. If Stump gave him free drinks, he invariably made them up in a generous tip. Prendergass, who lived in St. Louis, had won the Missouri lottery, had money to burn, and loved ND football. He also loved the fun and fellowship he found at Corby's and with Stump. When he arrived, he would typically give Stump two hundred dollars to cover his anticipated drinking needs for his three day trips to South Bend. Joe Corby did not have many patrons who paid in advance.

Prendergass drove up seemingly every Thursday. Employed at a St. Louis newspaper, Prendergass was a walking encyclopedia and he possessed wisdom about life which Stump soaked up whenever he could. God, why couldn't Dad have been like John Prendergass?

Stump recalled that one day after closing, Prendergass bought him and Mac breakfast and gave him a ride home. When he shook hands with Prendergass, Stump was greeted with a hundred-dollar bill when he loosened his grip. Stump credits Prendergass with inspiring him to always work hard and never dodge a check. It has been a mantra I have also preached to my five kids all these years. When the check comes, don't ever have short arms. If you eat or drink, you reach for the check. If you can't afford that, don't go in the first place.

The years at Notre Dame were wonderful years for Stump. After making the golf team as a walk-on, Stump enjoyed a storied career. He set the course record at the old ND Golf Course, a sizzling sixty-four. It will never be broken, nor will his tournament record of eighteen under par. Why? Because due to the ever-expanding needs of the university, real estate covering nine holes was usurped a few years ago to accommodate new buildings for higher education.

In his senior year, Stump took a marketing course from Professor Vincent Raymond. He loved Raymond and had volunteered at a favorite handicap center of the good professor. Part of the senior year academic requirement was the need to write a thesis on a famous person. Political figures and activists were favorite subjects. Stump went another direction: he chose the wine magnate, Ernest Gallo. He certainly knew about his products.

At Notre Dame, drinking alcohol was a major part of the social scene in the 1970s. While the school is rightfully known more for its prestigious accomplishments and contributions, the social life of South Bend, Indiana doesn't exactly mirror that of urban schools like UCLA. On weekends, after a week of pounding the books, a large majority of us couldn't wait for the weekend parties to begin. For Stump to do his final research paper on an icon in the alcoholic beverage industry seemed a fitting way to conclude four years of partying and bartending.

I remember an article from our college days in the early 1970s from *Playboy*. Someone clipped it out and gave it to me. Alright, I looked at the entire issue. OK, a few times!

Anyway, while *Playboy* featured a bevy of beautiful, scantily clad or unclad beauties, it also often contained articles that were actually often interesting to read (although I don't remember any hung up in dorm rooms).

One article I am sure the administration didn't think was a resume builder. However, it evoked great pride in the vast majority of the Notre Dame student body that partied hard. The article ranked the top ten "party schools" (read universities/colleges). As I recall, names like Tulane, Virginia, and Colorado State were mentioned (the latest poll has the University of Wisconsin at Madison at the top!).

But in the ranking I saw more than thirty-five years ago, there was a big asterisk next to the number one ranking. After scrolling down to the bottom to find out why there was an asterisk, I further recall that it said something to this effect: "Please note the aforementioned schools do not include the only professional drinking school in the country: the University of Notre Dame." *(Here come the Irish!)*

In South Bend, Indiana, particularly in the winter, the social life of many revolved around boozing. Concoctions like "Whoppatoola," a combination of various fruit drinks and whatever cheap alcohol could be found, would often complement the ample supply of cases or kegs of Stroh's, Old Milwaukee, Busch, or other popularly priced beers.

Memories of drinking marathons like "case of beer day" "dirt week" or the "canoe races" are still vivid. But, those days are over. Senior Bar, located adjacent to the football stadium, has been renamed Legends and I am sure much to the delight of current president Father Jenkins, the student body enjoys a social life on a much higher plateau than we did.

Stump remembers those days well and he too participated in his fair share of drinking games at Notre Dame. Some took place at Corby's, some at the Senior Bar, some at keg parties. But Stump could always be relied upon to take on the big guys in a drinking contest. It was a way of life at Notre Dame.

When I worked for Anheuser-Busch, I used to love to go back to class reunions. Everyone would have their name tags on and invariably we all had to know what everyone else was doing for a vocation. Echoes of "I am a lawyer," "I am an investment banker," "I took over my father's business," "I am teaching and coaching," and "I am a doctor" were some of the responses to the occupational inquiries.

But when they asked me about my work, I used to love to respond, "I am in the beer business. Come to think of it, I am the only one I know who actually pursued his college major!"

We partied hard in South Bend but Stump remembers Notre Dame for so much more. Yes, we all had some great times and yes we all probably partied too much, but we learned how to be organized and we learned how to study. We also learned the value of giving back, how to win, and how to be inspired. We learned the importance of keeping Christ close in our lives. And we were proud to be a part of the class that produced the first woman valedictorian at Notre Dame, Marianne O'Connor.

We were proud to be disciples of one of the greatest clergymen in American History, Father Theodore Hesburgh, a man who has received more honorary awards from different corners of the world than any other clergyman I know – candidly, more than any other American I know.

Stump was so proud one day when he encountered Father Hesburgh on campus. He was floored when Father Hesburgh addressed him with, "Jimmy, how's it going?" He would go on to tell Jim how proud the university was of him, of his grades, his community help and summer work. Priceless!

While he had a flock of about six thousand students to look after, Father Hesburgh took the time to get to know as many as he could, personally. To this day, Jimmy gives "Father Ted" the credit for his lifelong quest for excellence and giving, and for always trying to remember the name of anyone he meets.

Back to Professor Raymond's class. When it came time to pick someone famous to write a thesis on, Stump thought like me: forget Nixon, McGovern, Mandella, and Mao. Stump decided to research an icon in the alcoholic beverage industry, Ernest Gallo.

When he started the paper, he thought the way to make a "rosé" wine was by simply blending whatever red and white wine you had behind the bar. During his research on Ernest Gallo, he learned a lot more.

Stump poured his heart into the paper. He wanted to finish his college with a bang. Expecting to be somewhat ridiculed for his subject matter, Stump was shocked to not only learn that he "aced" the paper, but that Professor Raymond actually knew Gallo and he had sent the paper to him.

Did Mr. Gallo enjoy it?

Enjoy it – he loved it! So much so that one day when Jimmy was working at Corby's just before the term ended, the phone rang. His buddy Mac picked it up, smiled and handed the phone to Stump, saying, "It's Ernest Gallo."

Stump, assured that one of his prankster friends was up to no good, reacted in a fashion similar to the way Annette Benning (as Sydney Ellen Wade) responded to her roommate in *The American President* when Michael Douglas' presidential Andrew Shephard called her at her home.

Stump proceeded to go off, berating the unsuspecting caller until he was enlightened firmly that this was Ernest Gallo himself!

Mr. Gallo was so impressed with the paper that he wanted to invite Stump to his winery in Modesto, California. Stump eagerly obliged. A corporate jet was dispatched to St. Joe's International Airport, and shortly thereafter, the diminutive James Kevin Culveyhouse was winging his way to Modesto.

Upon arriving he was given a welcome the likes of which he had not seen since he was heralded by his Merrillville, Indiana, fans after participating in the Biddy Basketball world championship some eleven years earlier.

Jimmy stayed in the Gallo home, was wined and dined, was given a private tour of the secret caverns where the real Gallo wine jewels were stored – the best bottles and vintages – and was ultimately extended a job offer to start with Gallo in Southern California. It was an adventure that few of us back in South Bend could believe the good fortune offered Jimmy until, shortly after walking across the stage to receive his diploma from his beloved Father Hesburgh, Jimmy Culveyhouse was back on the plane, soaring his way to the next chapter of this life as a salesman for the Gallo Winery.

While Jimmy had to finance one hundred percent of his college education, he was pleasantly surprised that he was presented with a graduation gift from his mom and dad. Knowing Jimmy would be abandoning the bib overalls for more formal work attire, Jimmy was thrilled to receive a brand new suit. It wasn't an expensive one. It didn't need to be. But it allowed him to take off on the next phase of his life with good thoughts of his dad.

Stump reflected on what Notre Dame meant to him. Although I knew little about him at the time, his website, www.jimculveyhouse. com, offers insight from Jim's perspective about his journey to Notre Dame. The desire to attend Notre Dame had driven Jimmy ever since he was a kid, growing up less than a hundred miles away from South Bend. To get to Notre Dame was an easy drive. But to get *into* Notre Dame – it took beating a lot of odds.

"My story with Notre Dame probably started out differently than most. I was declined admission three times, which was devastating as Notre Dame was the only school I ever wanted to attend, living only one and half hours away. My high school counselor, John Coggins, (Currently Dean of Students at Purdue University North Central) and an ND admission board member, Myron Busby, were both very disappointed as we had planned all of my high school activities and curriculum to make me a "well rounded student"... exactly what Notre Dame said they were looking for.

"I lettered in three sports, earning nine total letters, and was elected to the Andrean High School Hall of Fame for Golf and Tennis. I graduated with a B-plus average, was involved in a variety of charity work, and even volunteered for dance committees that were not exactly my cup of tea. After my three denials, I was given the opportunity to appear before the whole admission board and tell my story. I was not bashful. It must have worked as after I got home I received a call that I would be admitted as a probationary student. That meant I had to keep a B average my freshman year. The rest is history and I graduated in 1976 with a higher GPA than I had in high school.

"This was the first of many ways where Notre Dame helped shape my life. Never give up and give it everything you've got at all times. To pay for my freshman year, I tarred basements in the summer, one of the worst jobs imaginable. On campus I became the manager of the pool hall. I also tried out as a walk on for the golf team that had six returning starters. I played well enough to secure a spot and won a few tournaments and earned a monogram. The biggest event that will forever remain with me was one late Sunday night while walking back from the Rock to Flanner Hall (where I lived) I was stopped by someone who said, "Hi Jim, I just wanted to tell you how well you are doing in golf and in the classroom. We're proud of you." I turned and who was it but Father Hesburgh, the President of Notre Dame and my hero. He was the person who probably made the biggest impact on my life. We talked awhile and I was on cloud nine.

"Money was always an issue as I had no help. During the summers of my sophomore and junior ND years, I was a caddie master where I started caddying when I was ten years old. I also worked a very physical job, on the midnight shift, of a loading dock for a shipping company. I virtually didn't sleep from Tuesday morning to Saturday morning all summer. But I would have done anything to keep being able to attend Notre Dame. Look at just the sports moments: the Sugar Bowl National Championship against Alabama, the ending of UCLA's basketball streak, and all the great comebacks and thrills I was able to witness as a ND student. I worked my junior and senior years at a local bar as a bartender and at 2:00 a.m. was a short-order cook until 3:00 a.m. I still attended all my classes and monogrammed all four years in golf and had many great experiences as a ND athlete."

A lot is made of the "spirit of Notre Dame." It is a special place for those of us who attended. Sometimes I get a bit upset when I see "subway" alumni (those who did not go there but wish they did) make a scene at games or social gathering places. They give all alumni a black eye. There just doesn't seem to be any gray areas when it comes to opinions on Notre Dame. People either love it or hate it. Alumni arrogance plays a key role in how others view "Our Lady." Indifference to Notre Dame does not seem to exist.

I enjoy reading the Notre Dame alumni communications or Monogram Club epistles. There are about a hundred and twenty thousand alumni from Notre Dame. It is amazing to see what many have gone on to do. The Hesiman Trophy winners are top of mind for most. But I also love knowing that graduates include talk show hosts Phil Donahue and Regis Philbin; former Secretary of State, Condoleeza Rice; sports personalities Mike Golic and Hannah Storm; San Francisco 49ers owner Edward DeBartolo; astronaut Jim Wetherbee; the great Knute Rockne; prolific novelist Nicholas Sparks – you get the idea. A lot of people have gone on to do a lot of good things.

Most of us have not achieved such notoriety. Nevertheless, it does not minimize the accomplishments of those who toil to make a difference in the lives of those in need.

Gary "Goose" Novak, a classmate and fellow basketball player, was an Academic All-American. He became a doctor. Not one of those world-class surgeons but rather your local neighborhood internist. He works out of a small office in a strip mall in Wilmette, Illinois. He does not charge for all of the senior nuns he sees. Heck, it would be my guess that "Goose" undercharges anyone he thinks might be in a bad way. He is a hero in my mind, an excellent example of what a Notre Dame man is all about.

Al Sondej graduated with us. Built like the proverbial brick you-know-what house, his muscles always bulged as if they were going to pop. I was afraid some day someone was going to tear him down and put up a parking lot in his place. He was huge. His presence with his flowing blond hair can still be felt, and his booming laugh still echoes around the North Quad Dining Hall at Notre Dame.

He lived in the firehouse of the campus fire department and when he wasn't in class or at the gym pumping iron, he was a volunteer fireman along with the infamous football player, number sixty-nine, Ed "Duke" Scales. While Duke and the rest of us were spending our off-season casual time and money on such worthy adventures like "case of beer day," "the canoe races," or "dirt week," Al decided to put his partying days behind him. He started putting the money he would have spent drinking aside and created a fund to feed the hungry. Big Al could be seen every day at lunchtime, standing outside the North Dining Hall with a large canister. Rain, snow, or shine, he would stand there quietly and would accept any contributions he received. Each week Al would send the money off to feed the poor. He raised thousands of dollars from others and he gave thousands of his own money for those who needed it.

After graduating, while the rest of us went to work trying to make our fortune, Al pursued his dream. He volunteered for the Hyattsville Fire Department. Not a lot of money (the word "volunteer" kind of gives that away). He did it because he loved it; he did it because it needed to be done. But in 1988, in late January, bad things happened. From the Hyattsville Volunteers website:

"On this day (January 27, 1988) twenty-one years ago, Firefighter Al Sondej entered a burning house at 2020 Wardman Road in Avondale as part of the crew of Truck 1 for a report of people trapped. As Al was searching, flames suddenly engulfed the room and Firefighter Sondej.

"It was later determined the lone occupant had escaped the house just prior to Sondej's arrival. Sondej received burns over most of his body and was transported to the Washington Hospital Center MedStar Burn Unit with third-degree burns. He remained there until his death on March 16, 1988 from burn complications."

I wasn't there for Al. I never knew about it. I never visited him where he lay in a hospital bed for more than a month and one half in pain none of us can imagine.

Al did not have to go into that house. In fact, there was no one in there. He gave his life because there was a chance someone was in there. Al is a hero to me. I only wish I had been there for him.

That is the way I feel about Jimmy. I am three time zones away and I can't physically be there for Jimmy but I can at least try to tell his story. Since he graduated from Notre Dame, he has given so much, of himself and for others. And in the last five years, he has endured pain few of us know – prostate cancer, Hepatitis C, and now ALS. But you never hear him complain.

Not able to walk and now incapable of speaking, Stump never stops in his quest. He just keeps on trying to raise money for ALS research – three hundred thousand dollars and counting. He and his wife Melanie just adopted their two teenage nieces, Parvaneh (Pari for short) and Sarah, after Melanie's sister, Tina, died from cancer. They brought them to Salem, Oregon, where they are trying to give them a better life. There are givers and there are takers in this world. Jimmy and Mel are givers extraordinaire.

Jimmy is a hero to me. He is a man who stands tall in the eyes of so many he has helped along his way, at Gallo, at Coke, and at Chemeketa Community College. His journey has been littered with funny stories and improbable outcomes to head-shaking situations. He has also endured his fair share of tragedy. But he has inspired thousands with his care and his teachings. Jimmy is a fighter and he is a giver. He is a teacher and he is one of the best salesmen this planet has ever seen. Jimmy credits Notre Dame for molding the man he is today.

Jimmy's Updates

I was so moved by Mitch Albom's *Tuesdays With Morrie* as he spent many Tuesday afternoons with his favorite professor, learning life's lessons from the mind of a very wise man. He chronicled the deterioration of Morrie and you could not help but be struck by the candor and how insightful Professor Schwartz was as death crept into his body.

Jimmy has taken a similar step of giving all of us the opportunity to read what usually amounts to monthly updates about what it is like to live with ALS. On Jimmy's website (www.jimculveyhouse.com) he provides regular updates about his condition as well as the status of the fundraising efforts. Sometimes Melanie will pen the update because Jimmy has had a setback. As always, one of Jimmy's brothers-in-law, Alex Herzog, faithfully updates the website.

Since I have reconnected with Jim, there have been several updates. They are interspersed throughout the rest of the book. They give you an idea of not only the determination of Jimmy to do everything he can to raise money for ALS research, but also you get the painful reality of the progression of his illness.

March 17, 2008 Update – Happy St. Patrick's Day!
(from Jimmy's web-site www.jimculveyhouse.com)

First of all, if you could all say a little prayer for my Mom in Phoenix, it would be much appreciated as she has gone through two brain surgeries in the past two weeks.

This week will be a busy one. Two of my darling nieces, Sarah and Pari, are coming Tuesday for nine days from Guadalajara to visit. My sister Shawn, her husband Alex (my "Webmeister," he's German!), five-year-old nephew Prescott, and my ten-month-old goddaughter Aubree are coming Wednesday to spend Easter with us. A packed house but it will be great having family around. The only negative is Melanie broke her foot Thursday and is in a cast for six weeks. Boy, what a pair we are!

I'm doing OK, good days and bad days, but the fundraising really keeps me going. We have now surpassed $250,000 and with four events on the drawing board, two booked. We are excited about the future.

On April 30th, my good friend (and best man in our wedding) Jim Terry from Coca-Cola is sponsoring a golf event at my club Creekside here in Salem. Dana Londin, our head PGA pro, has spearheaded the event and it's going to be a blast as well as a big fundraiser. Twenty of the top PGA pros in Oregon will be playing a two-man alternate shot "shoot out," securing pledges from members of their clubs. The event is open to the public with free admission. We're all excited about it and can't thank Dana enough for spending so much time on making it a success… and special thanks too to Oregon's own PGA great, Peter Jacobson, who designed Creekside and who has been a terrific support to me.

I want to wish everyone a safe and Happy Easter Weekend. In the spirit of St. Patrick's Day an old Irish Proverb for you:

"May you live as long as you want, and never want as long as you live!"

The Gallo Winery and Rich Mesnick

Jimmy's work career began at Gallo.

A couple of days after graduating, Jimmy flew to Los Angeles to begin his work career with Gallo Wines. He started out as a merchandiser but was quickly promoted to salesman, responsible for ensuring that Gallo products enjoyed prime shelf position in both grocery and package stores.

Headquartered in Modesto, California, and founded about seventy-five years ago by brothers Ernest and Julio Gallo, in the 1970s, Gallo was all about popular blends sold at a great price. Who will ever forget Chablis, Hearty Burgundy, Rosé, and Rhine wines? Their training programs were also legendary.

In 1975 after playing a year of pro basketball in Belgium, I had gone to work in sales for the Procter & Gamble Distributing Company, also renowned for great sales disciplines. Dressed in my three-piece suit, when I carried my sales bag into grocery stores, I felt like a Marine, that certain sense of being with the elite. There was only one other sales organization that carried that type of prestige and respect at retail and they were "from the vineyards of Ernest and Julio Gallo" (loved that voice of Orson Welles).

Gallo's sales structure was rigid and the penalties for not adhering to it were severe. Turnover could be high in some markets. I remember having dinner with some colleagues, including one of my managers, when we were comparing sales teams in the 1970s and the subject of Gallo arose. I said something respectful about Gallo and one of the junior sales people, very much full of himself and trying to impress the boss, blurted out, "Nobody stays with Gallo."

The boss looked at him and responded, "The good ones do."

How do you like them apples?

Jimmy not only impressed his superiors with his sales results, he wowed them with his creativity. Not happy with the limited merchandising space in the crowded wine section, Jimmy convinced some store managers to allow him to erect end aisle Gallo displays in other sections of the store, near chips and other impulse items.

Always meticulously organized, the minute merchandiser established a reputation for excellence. He loved the structure of the Gallo sales call regimen, but he had a boss that provided the latitude he needed to use his creative juices.

Rich Mesnick was Jimmy's first career mentor. As head of the Southern California Gallo sales office, it was "Mez" who bore the burden of the largest wine market in the U.S. for Gallo. Jimmy had been hand-selected by the man himself, Mr. Gallo. This kid had better be good, Mez thought to himself when his newly hired gun walked through the door. Mez was a rabid UCLA fan. He couldn't believe Mr. Gallo was going to saddle him with a Notre Dame graduate.

Jimmy had a bit of James Cagney in him. He learned a lot of lessons along the way to Gallo. Undersized, he knew that in order to win respect, you need to project confidence.

Confidence was one character trait in which Jimmy was not lacking, and it could easily be mistaken for cockiness. Whenever Mez would ask special assignments of Jimmy, he always received the same response: "No problem." And as Mez remembers, the kid always delivered.

Their professional relationship soon blossomed into a full-blown friendship. Mez loved golf, and what better companion to show up with at industry golf tournaments than the guy who holds the course record at Notre Dame.

In those days, and I guess probably now, there were few people in LA not connected with the Notre Dame family who approved of Notre Dame in pretty much any shape or form. People like my freshman roommate and eventual Senior Class President, Jerry Samaniego, left LA to attend Notre Dame. He and all others who matriculated to South Bend were total and unequivocal traitors.

When Jimmy was in school and even still today, Notre Dame's biggest two teams were men's football and men's basketball. The number one rivalry at that time in football was Southern California, and the biggest rivalry in NCAA basketball was without a doubt Notre Dame vs. UCLA. Both rivalries were southern California teams, located just a few miles apart in Los Angeles. They hated each other, but they both seemed to despise Notre Dame more.

It did not help matters any that Notre Dame often got the best of their California counterparts in the early 1970s. Notre Dame had won the national football title Jimmy's sophomore year, a year which included a big win over the Trojans. Not even the wild comeback led by Anthony Davis' five touchdowns in the fall of 1974 could erase the memories of Eric Penick's eighty-two-yard touchdown run in 1973 to help upset USC and win the title. Notre Dame would bounce back and win another national title in 1977.

On the hardwood, UCLA's dominance of college basketball in the 1960s and early 1970s was perhaps the greatest dynasty of a major sport in college history, certainly hoops. They enjoyed a winning streak that covered three seasons, from 1971 to 1974, some eighty-eight games. Names like Sidney Wicks, Curtis Rowe, Bill Walton, David Meyers, Keith Wilkes, Tommy Curtis, Pete Trgovich, Swen Nader, and Marques Johnson. John Wooden commanded a lock on the top talent in the country and this was *after* the Lew Alcindor era.

The last team to beat UCLA in hoops before they took off on their winning streak was, you guessed it, Notre Dame during my freshman year, in January 1971. Austin Carr's forty-six points as well as Collis Jones' monster defensive efforts and inside scoring led the way.

Oh, and the team to break UCLA's eighty-eight game winning streak, three years later? Notre Dame, highlighted by a furious comeback. Down eleven points with 3:22 to go, Digger called a timeout and he made us believe we could still win. The Irish then scored the last twelve points of the game. John Shumate, Gary Novak, Adrian Dantley, the incomparable Gary Brokaw, and the Iceman, Dwight Clay. Who will forget Iceman's jumper from the corner falling away into the stands? Swish!

Even though we were both undefeated at game time, most thought the Bruins were invincible. It was number two Notre Dame versus number one UCLA on national TV. Digger made us believe we could do it and we did.

Two years later it was 1976. Yet I am sure UCLA Bruins fans still remembered the call of Dick Enberg in those last furious seconds when UCLA tried to score as Bill Walton, Pete Trgovich, and David Meyers all had close shots at the hoop. I know Stump remembered it.

Enberg's call: "In to Walton... he can't score... Trgovich... Meyers... Shumate and the number-one-ranked UCLA Bruins have been upset by the Irish of Notre Dame seventy-one to seventy. The longest winning streak in collegiate sports history has ended where it began three years ago." Kind of warms the heart, doesn't it?

When I tell this story and people know I was on that team, I often hear, "I remember you from that game!"

I then mumble to myself, "Not unless you recognize the back of my head." I didn't get in that game but I was happy to be a part of that historic team.

When we knocked off UCLA, it occurred less than twenty-four hours after the Irish hockey team led by Ric Schafer, Eddie Bumbacco, Mark Kronholm, and the late Bill Nyrop knocked off number one Michigan Tech, seven to one. It was also only twenty days after the Irish won the National Championship in football, in an equally thrilling win at the Sugar Bowl on New Year's Eve by a score of twenty-four to twenty-three. It was a game that Howard Cosell described as the greatest college game he had ever seen. With the UCLA win, it marked the first time since they started keeping the AP polls that the same university stood atop both the football and basketball polls at the same time.

The Fighting Irish of Notre Dame.

Stump was there for the hockey team's win, he was there for the Sugar Bowl win, and, yep, Stump was courtside when we broke the streak. He was at every major Irish game and with a memory like an elephant he never tired of pouring it on Southern California sports fans. Then to make matters worse, in the golf tournaments, much to the delight of his mentor, he would often back up his bragging by shooting some ridiculous sub-par score while enjoying a few relaxing libations. The nineteenth hole would be too much to bear for many locals. The kid from Notre Dame was something else and he never tired of rubbing in the success of his beloved Irish on any Trojan or Bruin fan.

Over time, the retailers and his Gallo co-workers took a huge liking to the cocky little kid from Gary, Indiana. He not only talked the talk. He walked the walk.

Mez loved Jimmy. They played golf together, made sales calls together on the toughest of accounts, and partied together. The laughs were plentiful and the memories vivid. Sitting in a lounge in Las Vegas where he currently lives, Mez remembered his friend and the stories as if they happened yesterday. He stated, "I have never met anyone who has so much life in him and someone who is so fearless. He may be only five-foot-six but he has the swagger of a giant and he is my best friend. He has always been there for me and I will miss him like a brother."

After a year of breaking a bunch of sales records, Stump enjoyed a well-earned promotion to Northern LA District Manager in 1976. More record sales in a short time garnered him another promotion to the restaurant side of the business. In 1977, Jimmy was in his element, Restaurant Manager for Gallo Wines in San Luis Obispo, California.

It was in the restaurant side of the business where Jimmy really made his mark. Gallo wines would no longer be simply jugs to be found in grocery stores or liquor stores. With Jimmy Culveyhouse on the job, you would start seeing them in restaurants too.

His efforts did not go unnoticed. Later that year, Jimmy was packing his bags again. Next stop: the Caribbean, where he was to launch Gallo wines in Trinidad. Talk about a change of scenery. Gallo knew they had a salesman who did not understand the word

"No." If there was a way to sell a customer, Jimmy would find it, and Mr. Gallo wanted his best man to open up the Caribbean.

Jimmy became the Joe Girard of the wine business. For those for whom the name Joe Girard does not ring a bell, according to the *Guinness Book of World Records,* Joe Girard sold more cars than any other sales person ever: more than thirteen thousand cars sold at retail. His attention to detail and his inability to accept no for an answer are legendary. He makes a living now lecturing and selling off of his website. One of his tactics is to write birthday cards to anyone and everyone with whom he has done business.

Similarly, all of the almost five hundred people who have donated to ALS in Jimmy's name have received a personal thank you note from Jimmy. Not a quick e-mail, but a handwritten thank you note.

Jimmy was the Joe Girard of Gallo.

Jimmy's salesmanship was not limited to across-the-table selling. He could talk the paint off a Buick. He loved employing his communication skills on the ladies in the bars. Quick to establish credibility with bar owners, Jimmy would leverage that advantage by picking up the most beautiful and statuesque young women in Trinidad.

Jimmy dated a number of knockouts. One went on to become – yep, Miss Universe.

Now, I am sorry. If you don't think this kid could sell, how many lanky beauty queens date five-foot-six wine salesmen? Man, I wish I could have been a fly on the wall one of those nights when he waxed poetic into some lovely lady's ear.

Jimmy's time in Trinidad was relatively brief but he packed into that year what most people would do in a decade. 1978 was a very good year.

Not only did Stump date a future Miss Universe, he partied hard on two different occasions with the king of "reggae" music, Bob Marley. Additionally, when the world's most famous soccer player Pele played a World Cup game in Trinidad, who do you think ended up after the game as his running mate? My boy Jimmy... for an entire week!

On one occasion, while traveling from one island to another on what could only be called a puddle jumper, the pilot imbibed in one too many rum and Cokes. The result was that he was totally incapable of landing the plane. So who took over the controls of the plane and landed it without ever having taken a flying lesson? James Kevin Culveyhouse.

On yet another exciting venture, while landing on a quaint island named Mystique, the plane he was in encountered engine troubles as it completed its final approach. Somehow the pilot landed the crippled craft on its belly and Jimmy and the pilot jumped out of the craft just as it caught fire. They watched in disbelief from nearby bushes as the plane went up in flames.

Trinidad is only second in the world in carnival celebrations next to the most famous Rio Carnival. Night Train Express is the name of the wine Gallo launched in Trinidad and at carnival time, everyone needs good wine.

Jimmy explained to the Mr. Gallo that it would be much cheaper to rent an apartment than pay hotel rates. They agreed and Jimmy secured the penthouse view of the Carnival going past the judging stands and right in front of him. On the business side, Jimmy sold twenty-five CONTAINERS of Night Train Express wine that week. When he ordered the wine from the Modesto warehouse they were dumbfounded. And the Gallo management thought he was nuts. One, two, maybe three but *twenty-five* containers?

There is a rum shop on virtually every block of the island. Jimmy had the island covered ahead of time. Every parade participant who wanted wine could easily find Night Train Express for the big day. The inevitable happened – every bottle was sold. As Rich Mesnick says, "the world's greatest salesman had done it again". Twenty-five containers – gone and sold . Pretty amazing since less than nine months before, no one had ever even heard of the wine. Truly amazing from a truly amazing man!

While Jimmy secured placements of Gallo wines throughout the Caribbean and he enjoyed the social scene thoroughly, he also loved to take in the wonderful golf courses of the islands. The year he was there, he entered the Trinidad Open as an amateur and narrowly missed winning the whole thing despite the presence of scores of pro golfers. Second place never felt so good as Jimmy was the low amateur in the tournament by a mile.

Jimmy recalls his time in the islands as the most fun year of his life. It was a year even James Bond would envy as he participated in adventures of a lifetime. But all good things must come to an end. In between his social charades, Jimmy established Gallo wines as staples on every major bar menu and restaurant wine list. Mr. Gallo approved and once again picked up the phone to call his super salesman. There were new frontiers to conquer for the winery and Mr. Gallo wanted his best man to lead the charge.

After Trinidad, it was off to Denver where the focus of Jimmy's job was on-premise again (bars/restaurants). As the restaurant manager for the state of Colorado, Jimmy's objective was to secure as many placements of Gallo wines on the wine list as possible and get the "house pour" everywhere. "No problem," as Jimmy would say.

Gallo wines were barely on the map in those days, on-premise. Off-premise in grocery stores and liquor stores, they were dominant. But no one wanted Gallo Rhine Wine or Hearty Burgundy as the house pour; it just wasn't something you did – until Jimmy Culvey-house walked through your door.

Restaurant after restaurant converted to Gallo. More and more recruiters or "head hunters" were getting wind of this Gallo sales whiz, and Jimmy's phone started to ring.

It was about this time that the whole bar thing was wearing on Jimmy. He was a loyal guy, but he started to feel a bit used, and used up. He had done everything Mr. Gallo and the winery had asked of him – Southern California, Trinidad, Colorado. He had few regrets. He was ready for a change and he didn't want that change to be in Modesto.

When a recruiter called Jimmy about an opportunity at the world headquarters at Coca-Cola in Atlanta, Jimmy jumped at it. From the best in grapes to the best in beverages, Jimmy made the leap and accepted the job.

During the orientation process, Jimmy convinced his new employer, in an effort to gain an understanding of the business, to allow him to work in the field. The new manager agreed and Jimmy was diverted to Cincinnati, Ohio, where he would meet another lifelong friend and where he would meet his beloved Melanie.

The next chapter of Jimmy's life was about to begin... and it was "the Real Thing."

April 14, 2008 Update
(from Jimmy's website)

Mid-April is a special time for most kids involved in sports especially in the colder areas of the country and definitely if you are interested in track, tennis, baseball or golf. I was the same as any other kid growing up in Indiana. My sports were baseball and golf. No matter if there was still snow on the ground you went out and threw the ball around or hit some chip shots in the snow making believe it was sand.

For an aspiring golfer it can all be attributed to one event and especially one stretch of nine holes... The Masters... always the second week of April. The back nine on Sunday charges golfers up like no other "spring ritual" that happens every year.

Congratulations Trevor Immelman, this year's winner.

A lot of people have told me how sorry they feel for me that coming into the last third of my life that I won't be able to experience golf in my retirement. Don't feel sorry for me, I've had a great life and have been lucky enough to do a lot of those "retirement things" already. (If you still feel sorry, go to www.jimculveyhouse.com and make a donation to ALS even if it's $5.00.) Now I can spend the rest of what life I have to try and help others that are faced with my predicament. I just thank God for the things that I have been able to do. It's been a great ride!

Coca-Cola

Ahhhhh, the good old Midwest again. Cincinnati, Ohio. The Queen City is the center of the world for many Midwesterners. It was certainly perfect for Jimmy. From Cincinnati, it was only four and ½ hours home to Merrillville, Indiana, or South Bend, Chicago, or Cleveland; five hours to Detroit; and less than two hours to Churchill Downs. Jimmy was back in the Midwest and for him, it felt like Heaven.

It would be easy to now get back to the Bend for Irish home games. Traditional away games against Big 10 rivals Purdue, Michigan, and Michigan State would also be easy to make.

Most importantly, he could now get back to Merrillville to spend more time with his little sister, Shawn, who missed her brother a lot. Trips home from Trinidad and Denver were much less frequent. Jimmy always wrote or called but there was nothing like seeing her big brother come walking through that door.

And then there was mom and dad. With Nana gone, Jimmy worried a lot about his mom. Her drinking seemed to get progressively worse. But with his father still in a state of denial, there was little Jimmy could do. He felt badly for his mom. His dad had mellowed some over the years and he seemed to be a good dad for his sister and that was as much as Jimmy could expect. But it was primarily for Shawn that he returned to Merrillville.

Jimmy also never tired of returning to his alma mater, Andrean High School, as good a Catholic school as there is in the country. Jimmy earned nine letters at Andrean and was inducted into the Andrean Sports Hall of Fame not long after graduating. He used to love to wander the halls and visit the gym and the trophy case.

Northern Indiana was also the home of a man who was closer to Jimmy during his teen years than any other man, including his dad. Nick Thiros was an inspiration to Jimmy at Gary Country Club where he caddied for twelve years. Beginning when he was only ten years old, on many a weekend, young Jim would caddy for Nick and soak in the words of wisdom he would impart. Jimmy credits much of his success in life to this soft-spoken man who was so key to Jimmy developing needed life skills. If it wasn't for Nick Thiros, Jimmy believes he would have never made it into Notre Dame.

It was always good to see him and the feeling was mutual.

When Jimmy talks about Nick Thiros, his eyes light up.

"Nick was like a second father to me. I loved the man and I think the feeling was mutual.

"Nick and his lovely wife Helen were members of Gary C.C. There were a lot of colorful characters at the club and it was very important you remembered your place. Some were good tippers and some were not. Nick was a good tipper.

"By the time I was fifteen years old, I had become the top golfer at Andrean High. I owe so much to my caddying days at Gary. There is no one I owe more to than Nick. When the caddie pay rates were six dollars a round, Nick paid me twenty. When the minimum rates were raised to eight dollars, Nick would pay me forty. I loved caddying for either him with his friends or the afternoon rounds when he would play with Helen.

"Tanned and handsome, he was a man you just respected. He was a money player too. We weren't supposed to, but the caddies often bet on members and how they would play. I always bet on Nick, and I made a lot of money.

"I won a lot of tournaments over my life. However, no tournament I was involved in gave me more satisfaction than when the eight-handicap Nick Thiros won the Class A Championship with me on the bag.

"Nick not only tipped well, he taught well. We developed more of a father-son relationship than a golfer-caddie relationship. If he wanted to chip or putt, I would help him chip or putt. If he wanted to have lunch together, I would drop whatever I was doing to be in his company. He took an interest in me, a genuine interest. That is what dads do.

"James Culveyhouse was my father; Nick Thiros was my dad.

"Thanks, Nick, I hope to see you on the other side."

Jimmy would make the drive home, enjoy the weekend or at least a family Sunday, and then head back to Cincinnati. Those long drives gave him plenty of time to reflect on his life and on his new responsibilities.

At Coca-Cola, Jimmy was immersed into a new world. As the Mid-East advertising and promotions manager, Jimmy was free to promote Coke in virtually any way possible. With a generous advertising budget, Jimmy had more ideas than his managers had ever seen before. The regional manager of the Cincinnati office was a man who would also become a lifelong friend, Jim Terry.

J. T.

At six-foot-three, JT towered over Jimmy by close to a foot. He was senior to Jimmy at Coke and certainly had the authority to call the shots among the "Dynamic Duo." Batman and Robin, Tom and Jerry, Butch and Sundance, Abbott and Costello… all were legendary couplets. Each team had a clear leader and so did the tandem of "JT and JC" and it wasn't JT. The head of the James Gang when they hit the social scene in Cincinnati was my boy Jimmy.

An old picture of them cutting up together twenty-five years ago resurrected memories of Arnold Schwarzenegger and Danny De-Vito in the movie *Twins.* They just didn't look like a team, but they were inseparable.

"We both traveled quite a bit with our respective jobs at Coke. But if we were in town, we were together," JT mused with a distinct Southern drawl. "When it was quitting time, it was quaffing time."

Their escapades were legendary. Whether buying drinks for everyone they met at Friday's or "sprinkling the infield" at Christie's, another favorite watering hole, JT and Jimmy both could have used liver transplants after their time together in Ohio.

They had their own stools at Friday's, remembers Jimmy's future wife and Friday's bartender, Melanie. "When these two clowns came in, the party started."

They also took the show on the road as well. When Coke celebrated the launch of Diet Coke in Detroit at the Bonaventure Theatre, JT was there to party down with Stump. Jimmy was given a liberal budget to organize the celebration in the Motor City, and he created an event that will be forever remembered.

What a party: music, rear-screen projection, and celebrities. Jimmy corralled the hot CBS announcer Jayne Kennedy, Coke spokesman Mean Joe Greene, and legendary Michigan football head coach, Bo Schembechler, among others. Somehow, Jimmy even recruited the Michigan marching band that brought down the house by blasting the Diet Coke theme song marching down the aisles to start the show. The bars were rocking in Motown that trip and the James Gang were the lead posse.

There were other memorable moments for the thirsty twins. They took a bunch of customers to the Winter Olympics in Lake Placid in 1980. They hit all the events including the luge, bobsled, ski jumping, and naturally they were at center ice for the "Miracle on Ice," the U.S. team's thrilling win over the vaunted Russian hockey team. Few remember that was the semi-final game but one of the great moments in American sports history. They were back there when the U.S. won the gold medal too.

After the upstart hockey team won the gold medal against the Finns, the James Gang, armed with a generous entertainment expense budget, were the talk of the town in Lake Placid. The Olympic drink-a-thon was capped off by JT egging on Jimmy as he shimmied up a twenty-foot flag pole in the Olympic Village to "borrow" an Olympic flag. Jimmy still proudly displays it in his home office in Salem. I'm not sure when he plans to return it.

Jim Terry was the best man at Jimmy's wedding. He was complicit in the wedding party excursion which ended up at the Sting bar fifteen minutes before Jimmy's wedding was supposed to start. JT was the first one "Mez" approached with the crisis request that the groomsmen needed one last drink with the groom-to-be.

JT could have saved the day by not alerting Jimmy. Old habits die hard. He did. And it almost ruined the big day. Moreover, he still remembers he almost assured the disaster by locking the keys in the limo when they piled out of to get "one drink." He and Jimmy had cut a path through the singles bars of the Queen City like few before them and probably fewer after. The opportunity for one last mischievous bachelor adventure was too tempting to resist, even if it was fifteen minutes before the wedding. More about that later.

Jimmy would quickly receive a promotion to a sales management position in the Northwest U.S. Jimmy left Coca-Cola after he ran operations for sixteen NW Coke bottlers. It was what brought him to the state of Oregon. JT never left Coke. With thirty-four years experience, he is now vice president of national sales for the parent company. I can't even imagine what his portfolio of stock options looks like after all these years. Ironically, JT has recently endured his own personal health challenges. He is not out of the woods yet, but in a conversation with him in February 2009, he was more concerned about Jimmy than he was for himself.

Surprisingly, while they have stayed in touch, JT has seen Jimmy only one other time since he left Cincinnati more than two decades ago. That was at the Packers-Patriots Super Bowl game in 1996. A family gathering in Washington in July 2008, right where they filmed the movie *An Officer and a Gentleman*, brought JT to Jimmy's neck of the woods, north of Seattle. By coincidence, his trip coincided with my visit to see Jimmy in Salem. He was happy to make the drive down to see his old friend. It had been too long.

The years have been good to JT. Now sporting a shock of white hair, thoughts of John Madden came to mind when the burly Coke executive stepped through the door to the Culveyhouse home. Jimmy had taken an hour to freshen up and gather his strength so he could spend some quality time with his old friend.

Jimmy emerged from his bedroom with a big smile on his face, wearing a Los Angeles Dodgers game jersey with his name "Culveyhouse" printed on the back, a reminder of a story between the two of them. JT smiled and embraced his old friend. It was a long and warm hug. Jimmy is not much of a hugger but he wrapped his arms around JT's waist and it was long and sustained as if he didn't want to ever let him go.

The afternoon was memorable for them both. They reminisced about "the good old days." JT broke out photos of his beautiful identical twenty-two-year-old twins, now seniors at Auburn University. Jim had his collection of JT-related memorabilia organized as well.

The Atlanta-based JT also proudly showed off his Georgia Tech 1990 football national championship ring, presented to him by then head coach George O'Leary. JT has done so much for the Yellow Jacket football program that O'Leary presented him a ring, exactly like the one all the coaches and players received.

JT also presented Jimmy with a little surprise as he pulled out his membership card to Chrisie's, one of their favorite bars. It expired in 1982 but the memories were still strong.

Melanie and Jim broke out the wedding album and JT chuckled as he perused it with amazement as to how much he and Jimmy had changed and how much Melanie had not.

They looked at the photo of the small wedding party. On Jimmy's side, it consisted of the groom, Mez, JT, Mac, and one other person, Jerome "Ty" Taylor. The irony was not lost on them. Professor

Curme couldn't have calculated the odds of two of the five members of this wedding party developing ALS.

Ty Taylor died of ALS about seven years ago. Less than one in one hundred thousand get ALS. But forty percent of the Culveyhouse wedding party developed ALS only seven years apart. Who says lightening can't strike twice?

JT's family circle had endured its own tragedies; he revealed his seventeen-year-old niece had just passed away from bone cancer and the six-year-old of his best friend just died of a heart attack. It was a somber JT who had made this voyage to Salem.

JT had to depart for the long drive back to Washington. He was clearly moved by the visit. So was Jimmy. While he had not physically been to Oregon since Jimmy revealed he has ALS, he had ensured that Coke supported every ALS fundraising event initiated by Jimmy. JT would be back soon. They still keep in touch, but he wants more time with his friend. Jimmy is JT's best man, too.

Kicking off the month of May!
May 1, 2008
(from Jimmy's website)

"Most of you know my favorite expression is when you give you will always get twice in return. My payback came yesterday fourfold or more. The golf tournament "Coca-Cola presents the OPGA Shootout for ALS (Lou Gehrig's disease) hosted by Creekside Golf Club", my club, and Jim Culveyhouse, Founding Member and Oregon State spokesperson for the MDA-ALS division was a huge success.

There were 10 statewide PGA pros who participated in a golf shootout. They each had secured per hole pledges from their members on how far they could last. It was a wonderful event, fun to watch, the pros were great and a lot of "ribbing" went on. The best part was over $23,000 was raised for my cause – ALS research.

Today is a new day. Much more important is that it is a special day. Thousands of people read these updates. If I asked them what day today is, I'd bet not even 1% would know.

Today, May 1 is the start of ALS Awareness Month and our event yesterday was the kick off event. Why is it that people don't know of ALS Awareness Month? That's a good question and one that has bothered me for some time. Breast Cancer, Prostate Cancer (I know, I had it and beat it), MS, etc are all terrible things and people are aware of them. Few people are aware that ALS is also known as Lou Gehrig's disease. It was named after the famous Yankee ballplayer who was diagnosed in 1939 and gave a moving speech at Yankee Stadium. He died less than 2 years later. But what other famous people have died of the disease? Well, if you're a golfer you know of Bruce Edwards, Champion golfer Tom Watson's caddy. ALS has affected many more people than you might be aware of.

Let me list a few names you might have heard of:

Ezzard Charles, World Boxing Champion in 1950
David Niven, the actor
Lane Smith- the actor in "My Cousin Vinny"
Jacob Javitts, New York State Senator for 24 years
Jon Stone, Creator of Sesame Street
Eddie Adams, Pulitzer Prize winning photographer

Dennis Day, singer and TV personality and former "Mouseketeer"
Jim "Catfish" Hunter, one of baseball's great pitchers
Jason Becker, Rock guitarist with David Lee Roth
Jeff Julian, Professional Golf Association Golfer
General Maxwell Taylor, General Commander; US Army
Mao Tse Tung, Revolutionary leader of China
Henry Miller, Vice President in the Roosevelt Administration
Charlie Wedemeyer, NFL Football player
George Yardley, NBA Basketball Hall of Famer
Michael Zazlow, Emmy winning daytime actor
Wally Hilgenberg- Minnesota Vikings all-star

So why is this horrible, incurable, disease so little known and under funded? I have a close friend whose husband died of ALS. She's a smart lady that I respect and she finally gave me an answer that made sense and made me understand. ALS is incurable. Many other diseases are to some extent curable or can be treated. To date, ALS can't.

A patient with ALS has a very short life span after diagnosis. With most other diseases, there's at least a chance to be cured. If you were raising funds for yourself for a transplant or something similar, that's tangible. ALS is not, there is no current cure, and funds go to research which is intangible; big difference for people giving money.

Research is faceless. It doesn't pull at people's hearts the way making a donation to a face does. Research to a lot of people is too far removed. This close friend of mine has hit the nail on the head with my frustrations of how hard it is to secure donations. I understand it. I said she's one smart lady, Marcia Bagnall. Her husband, of Bryce Vineyards, Bryce Bagnall, died of ALS.

Bryce started a successful winery. He also took my course at Chemeketa. I remember him telling me: "Why do I need a consultant who doesn't know anything about fine wines?" After letting me talk to him for five minutes, he agreed to take the course and I am happy to say, he benefited from it. I became very close to Bryce, never knowing the same disease that struck him would attack me as well

In fact, in the last days before he died I visited him which Marcia would say later were special moments for him. Now, I look like Bryce did in the latter stages of his life.

That's why I'm including "current" pictures of me on the sight. I'm no longer that strong, athletic, full of life man, always "up" and ready to do anything, anytime. I am what I am, a guy who has lost over 30 pounds, has not eaten a solid piece of food in over a year, has a very difficult time walking, and is extremely hard to understand because of my slurred speech. I have very little stamina, and my passionate golf game is almost gone. I need a breathing machine while I sleep, etc. and all in all I feel my body deteriorating almost everyday. Those are the facts. I'm still "up" when I'm around people because I refuse to let this beat me down.

In the jobs I've had and contacts with friends and people I have given a lot of advice to them on a variety of matters. Now I'm asking for something in return, which isn't my style and you all know it if you know me at all. I appreciate all the people that have donated to my fundraising campaign to raise funds for research for this horrible, incurable, little known, under funded disease. They understand that it affects not only the inflicted one but their friends and families as well. This disease is a tough one emotionally for all around and extremely expensive. We have made in-roads but not what we should have since Lou Gehrig died in 1941. That's inexcusable for a great country like America.

I'm asking sometime this month to use a little of that tax refund you might have received, or that federal rebate that everyone is getting from the government, or go to one less movie, one less Starbucks, have one less good cigar, one less candy bar, one less cocktail, one less lunch out, one less pizza, etc. There are so many "little things" that you can easily give up just once or twice or three times throughout the month and give a donation to ALS research for $5 or $10 or $20 or more.

In my business career I dealt in people's personal and business cash flows understanding their inflow and outgo of money on a monthly basis. I never in all those years couldn't find something that every person could cut back on a little if they really wanted to. That's what I'm asking you to do for me. Remember whatever you give you get "twice in return".

Make yourself feel better and go to http://www. jimculveyhouse.com/ and give something. Everybody can do it... I'm hoping you do."

God bless.

Melanie

Melanie and Jim have been married for twenty-six years. They met at a T.G.I. Friday's in Cincinnati. Melanie was head of the bar and Jim was settling into his new Coke responsibilities at the time. He was smitten with her from the get-go, but Melanie was thoroughly unimpressed with a guy who seemed to be cockier than Muhammad Ali. Jimmy didn't go around bragging, "I am the greatest of all time." But Melanie certainly thought he acted that way.

There was no way she was going to go out with this guy.

But Jimmy had made up his mind. He and his fellow Coke manager JT were not just regulars at Friday's, they were almost a permanent fixture. They spent more time at the Friday's bar than Norm and Frasier did at Cheers. And, as Melanie recalls, their bachelor shenanigans were the stuff usually reserved for legends.

While Melanie would laugh with Jimmy, and occasionally share a drink, she continued to reject his overtures for a date.

Jim, however, had made up his mind. This was the girl of his dreams and he was going to be with her. He would prove to her she was wrong about him and that he was a good guy – that if they could be together, he could tame his wild side.

Melanie states that basically he just wore her down. The same dogged determination which had served him well in business eventually paid dividends with the apple of his eye. He used every selling skill he had. Actually, he basically conned her into the first date.

After a year and a half of hearing the word "no," Jimmy finally realized he had to alter his approach. The full frontal assault strategy just would not work on this hard-working Texas girl. So one day when he and JT had an extra ticket to the Bengals game, Jimmy approached Melanie with a different angle.

"Hey, I have an extra ticket to the Bengals game," he stated. "Ya wanna go? It's not a date. It's just a game. I have an extra ticket and I know you like football. JT and I are gonna be there with a few others. It'll be fun. No pressure. No date, just a game."

Melanie admitted she did love football, and tickets to the Bengals rarely fell into her lap. This was back in the days when the Bengals were good, very good. She acknowledged that she did think the two of them were a lot of fun and rationalized that it was not a date since she was basically going to an event with two of them.

The adjustment to the game plan worked and at the game Jimmy worked his charm and Melanie finally let her guard down. They have been together ever since.

After a courtship of appropriate length, Jimmy popped the question, and on March 26, 1983, they were married in Cincinnati. But it almost ended before it even started. Jimmy's good friend and former Gallo boss, Rich Mesnick, remembers it well.

"I was an usher in my best friend's wedding which was to take place at 5:00 p.m., Saturday night. At 4:40 p.m., two of the boys in the wedding party grabbed me and said, 'Richie, we need a drink.' I looked at my watch and said, 'Now?' And they said, 'We want one last drink with Jimmy while he is still a bachelor.' Before I could get the words out that the ceremony was in minutes, the look in their eyes told me of the urgency. NOW!!!

"I grabbed the best man (Jim Terry from Coca-Cola) and explained the situation. He grabbed Jimmy, the proud and serene groom-to-be and said, 'Jimmy, we have a problem. The boys want one last drink with you and they want one now!'

"Jimmy smiled that Cheshire cat smile and I knew we were in trouble when he uttered his infamous response, 'No problem.'

"And with that, Jim grabbed his father-in-law-to-be, and all the guys in the wedding party and we all piled into the limo. Remember it was 4:40, twenty minutes before the ceremony was to begin. Before the door was closed I told the driver to pull into the first bar he saw and that is exactly what he did.

"He raced down Columbia Parkway and pulled up to bar that resembled the Crow's Nest in the movie *The Perfect Storm*. We jumped out and in our formal glory, tuxes and all, we walked in to a real country tavern.

"The bartender looked and she deadpanned, 'Who died?'

"In one voice we pointed at Jim and said, 'He is about to be married in fifteen minutes.' And then, I continued, 'And we want one more drink with our boy before he takes the plunge!'

"I looked at my watch and the wedding was to start in fifteen minutes. The innkeeper ordered a round of drinks, shots and a beer for the bunch; and then announced that it's on the house. We all looked at each other and arrived at the same fateful conclusion that was to the effect of, 'Well, we can't bail on a house drink.'

"So we had to show respect and buy another round for the house and then for good measure a third. I looked at my watch and as if we were a collective Cinderella, I knew our coach had turned back into a pumpkin. It was 5:15 p.m. and we were in some deep do-do. So we then piled back into the limo and sped to the church with the limo driver shaking his head the whole time.

"We jumped out of the car, with our previously perfectly pressed tuxes now wrongfully wrinkled. Hoping that perhaps Melanie was running late, we all bounded up the steps. As suspected, waiting just inside the vestibule was the minister and the lovely bride to be.

"We filed past Melanie one by one with our heads slanted downward, some of us muttering our apologies as we passed. The stoic minister followed us in. The last to enter the church was the groom to be.

"Now Melanie has always had a great sense of humor. Born and raised in Texas, she is a tough lady but not without a mischievous side herself. But the expression on her face was clear. Someone was looking at a death sentence and it wasn't her dad who had the kind of look on his face like, 'I didn't do it – they made me do it.'

"As we took our places at the front of the church, you could feel the eyes of those assembled glaring through us all. Eye contact with anyone was avoided at all costs. The music played, and played, and played. It felt like the orchestra on the deck of the Titanic as it was going down. Seconds seem to turn to minutes and minutes seemed to be more like hours. It was so painful you thought you could time this delay with a calendar.

"Just as I was getting ready to start taking the bets with the ushers about whether or not this wedding was going to be called off on account of stupidity, I felt a loving tap on my shoulder. There was my boy Jimmy and as the organ began to play and the beautiful bride started down the aisle he winked at me and said, 'No problem.'

"Twenty-six years later, Melanie and Jim laugh at the event, but Melanie isn't shy about saying there was almost a homicide in the back of the church that day. I thought it was over and would have given odds. Jim could have made a lot of money taking those bets!"

Melanie has always been there with and for Jimmy, and Jimmy always tries to make her feel special.

For Melanie's fiftieth birthday, Jimmy wanted to do something memorable for her. Ever the one to be able to make the improbable occur, here is how Jim describes the surprise.

> *"I have always tried to get Melanie great gifts for very special occasions or if I have the opportunity to do something really unique, I will, like playing Pebble Beach on the exact day of her 50th birthday. It's the one course she said she'd like to play if she won the lottery more than any other in the world. I have others but I love the story about the Los Angeles Lakers.*
>
> *Melanie was a huge Lakers fan during the "Showtime" years, which is amazing because as she will admit growing up she had no interest in sports at all until meeting me. Well that team; Magic, Kareem, Cooper, Rambis, Worthy, etc. she just clung to. I think she watched almost 75% of the games every year.*
>
> *Kareem's last year, (forget the year) if you remember, was a farewell tour where everywhere he went they had a pre-game presentation and gave him something. Boston gave him a piece of the parquet floor. Other teams did something special too.*

Working for Coke I did a lot of things with the Trailblazers and we were one of their main sponsors. Through my "moles" I found out that Larry Weinberg, who owned the Blazers then and lived in LA, was not going to be there for the game on Friday night, Kareem's last road game of his career.

Sooooo I sucked it up and used up every favor and got his floor seats. Well when you're in the owner seats you can show up as early as you want, so we did. Melanie was decked out in a Lakers hat, Lakers sweater, Lakers pants, Lakers shoes and a Lakers pennant,

... IN THE TRAILBLAZER OWNER'S SEATS!!!!

All the Lakers came over to meet her and she explained what a fan she was and they said we must be the only Laker fans in Portland. We laughed and they just kind of hung around us and talked while they were warming up. We watched the game and when one of the Lakers would come off the bench to go into the game, he'd always look over and give her a wink. It was the perfect birthday for Melanie but it was just starting.

The next day we flew to LA and I told her we were visiting friends (Mesnick)...partly true... but Sunday was the best of all. I had purchased the two tickets behind Jack Nicholson at the start of the year for $600 (they would be $20,000 today). I had secretly packed her Lakers gear. This was Kareem's last regular season game. We went way early and when the team came out for warm-ups, who do they see but Melanie dressed in her gear and me again as we were sitting right there at mid-court. They all came over and gave her a kiss, said she was the No.1 Lakers fan and let her come out on the court while they were warming up.

There was a lot of hoopla. Kareem got a big rocking chair, his family and friends were there, and the TEAM chipped in and bought him a gold Rolls Royce. At the end of the first quarter, I had a smoke with Jack Nicholson and talked to him for about 10 minutes. At halftime, he took us to a special room that owner Jerry Buss has and ate and drank. After the game Jack and the team invited us to Kareem's going away party that was for family, a few close friends, the team and their families. To say it was the experience of a lifetime is an understatement, definitely one you'll never forget and I love doing that type of thing for Melanie... she so deserves it."

Jimmy refers to his bride of twenty-six years as his guardian angel. And after spending time in her presence, I so understand why. There is an ebullience about Melanie that is hard to describe. A "strawberry blond" with beautiful blue eyes, she never seems to rest until everyone is happy. She is an amazing cook and the home she keeps seems to scream "Welcome."

Both Melanie and Jim are very organized. Their yard looks like it belongs in *Home and Garden* with colorful flowers, manicured bushes, and a lawn which could be a model for Scott's Turf Builder. The recent addition of a unique "butcher block" water fountain is just the latest addition to an inviting backyard.

Melanie has endured pain before. Though both her mom and dad are still alive, she lost one of her sisters, Tina, to breast cancer three years ago. Tina's husband, Majid, lives in Guadalahara, Mexico. Tina left behind two beautiful teenage daughters. Pari is now eighteen and Sarah is fifteen. They love to visit Jim and Melanie and did so twice in 2008, including August where they were a wonderful part of a surprise birthday party for Melanie, somehow engineered by the ever-scheming but always thoughtful Jimmy.

After attempting to adjust to life in Mexico versus San Antonio, where they were raised prior to their mom's death, the girls were elated when Melanie and Jim offered to have them live with them. They love helping support Melanie with Jim's care and they have more poise and elegance than any two sisters their age I ever remember meeting.

Pari is finishing high school with her sites set on attending either Oregon University, University of Washington, or Notre Dame. Elegant, confident, and graceful, Pari is wise well beyond her years.

Sarah is just as nice at they come. Changing environments early in high school is a challenge for anyone. Sarah has handled the transition with amazing maturity. She is driving now and her opportunities in the future are limitless.

So Melanie is now the mom she always hoped to be. Funny how things work. As she battles to make Jim's remaining days with her as comfortable as they can be, she also now has the privilege of parenting two wonderful girls.

Melanie has immersed herself into Jim's care. A former president of the Women's Group at Creekside, she shares Jim's passion for golf. She also has become active in ALS support groups for families just starting to deal with the shock of the disease. She laughs freely and always seems to be upbeat. Her attention to detail is amazing. Melanie is the epitome of a "giver" and without lovely Mel, Jim's trip toward the darkness would be unbearable.

May 27, 2008

(From Jimmy's website)

Medical Update on Jim
by Melanie

"We thought it was time for another medical update on Jim. It's been 16 months since Jim's diagnosis. One doctor thought he would be gone by now (he didn't know Jim!!). The ALS has taken its course the way it wanted. It has progressed as they thought it would but on it's course, or maybe I should say, Jim's course.

Our quarterly appointment with OHSU went as expected; everyone noticing that Jim's speech had declined substantially. So visiting with Melanie Fried-Oken, the speech pathologist was our priority. It is time for an augmentative communication device so we will visit her again in mid-June to be "fitted" for the proper computer. It will save Jim energy and his voice for when he needs it.

The ALS is causing the nerves in Jim's diaphragm to die, thus rendering his muscles useless. Without diaphragm muscles outside equipment is necessary to breathe. At night, Jim is using a V-Pap machine which breathes for him. He now has to use it during the day sometimes when he gets tired. All of his doctors think by using both the V-Pap, and the speech device it gives Jim more energy to use for the things he loves to do.

Dr. John Silver, Jim's pulmonologist, will be his primary local Salem doctor from now on. Keeping Jim breathing and his lungs healthy are our main goals. What's really great is Dr. Silver will also take care of Jim's feeding tube!! Who Knew? (In case it becomes infected or needs to be changed) He also ordered another new machine for

Jim that is called a "Cough Assist". Because Jim is unable to cough he cannot get the extra fluid and mucus out of his lungs. This machine will do that for him. (Linacre, a home medical equipment provider, is great. They have taken very good care of Jim).

There is an entire regimen of things we do each day to keep Jim healthy and happy. So, FYI, I have attached a daily schedule to give you an idea of what we do.

Time - Jim's Daily Medical Needs:

7:00a Administer morning drugs through tube
7:30   Change feeding bag to 500ml water, set rate at 500ml/hour
8:00
9:00   Use Nebulizer
10:00 V-Pap if necessary, Cough Assist machine
11:00
12:00p Administer noon drugs through tube
1:00   V-Pap if necessary
2:00   Use Nebulizer
3:00   250ml food and water through tube
4:00
5:00   Use Nebulizer
6:00
7:00   V-Pap if necessary; Cough Assist
8:00
9:00   Administer evening drugs through tube
10:00
11:00 Hook up 1500 ml enteral bag for night time feeding, and V-Pap
Good Night

Jimmy continues…

"That was at the end of May. Since then I have lost more stamina, get tired much quicker, and have trouble walking even with a brace on my left leg. For an energetic, sports nut and dedicated golfer this was deeply depressing but I tried not to show it. Other people have problems too, I did my self pity mourning by myself and there was plenty.

I sleep a lot because of my loss in stamina. I have tripped a few times because my left leg gives in and my left toes curl up and down as I go. I used to be an early morning riser but I can't get up until at least 9AM for the drugs and water to finish going through my feeding tube. I read the paper, have some coffee and hope my bowel movements work as that is a big problem also. I do keep my spirits up by treating every day like it's a regular work day. I have my lists and I try to accomplish as much as I can. I usually tire out in the afternoon, take a nap and try to take in some more liquid food and water while I'm sleeping. I'm pretty used to it now but at the beginning it was real tough smelling the aromas of good food and not being able to eat. It's been 16 months since I've had solid food.

On the days proceeding the 4th of July I was feeling a little depressed as we had some of our family fly in and they were all going over to see the fireworks. I didn't want to stay up that late or make the trek over to see them…

ALS sucks… Gosh I wish I could just play some golf!

Golf

Golf – what a game. It is the most difficult, humbling game ever played. As an athlete, I figured I would pick golf up when I felt like it and would learn it in no time. Unlike Jimmy, I did not grow up on a golf course and I so regret that.

I played the "jock" sports: football, basketball, and baseball. When I was growing up, anyone who played golf, tennis, or the piano was a "wuss."

Now? I would die to do any of the three well.

Having coached all of my kids in hoops at one time I encouraged them to be well balanced and to learn other sports. I cannot yet get my daughter, Riley, on the course, but my sons, Patrick, Casey, Conor and Peter, all swing the sticks well.

The nice thing about golf is that you really can play the game your whole life. Melanie and Jimmy played all the time together in between Jimmy's competitive rounds. With the beauty of the handicap system, any two players can enjoy some friendly competition. The banter of giving or getting strokes can sometimes be half of the fun.

President Woodrow Wilson stated: "Golf is an ineffectual attempt to place an elusive ball into an obscure hole with implements ill-adapted for the purpose." No truer words were ever spoken.

Jimmy has always been good at golf. I have not.

I remember when I first started to play. Like baseball, I thought the object of the game was to swing as hard as you could. How else was that little white ball going to end up three hundred yards down the fairway? Even some twenty years later, I still can't seem to process it. There isn't enough Ritalin in the world to get me to focus and remember when I am standing over the ball that speed, power, and quickness, while laudable attributes for other sports, have nothing to do with success on the links.

Golf is all about tempo, balance, and finesse – and integrity.

In my freshman year at Notre Dame, we had to take a gym class one semester. Part of that class featured a day with the golf coach. I will never forget his advice: "There are two things you need to learn how to do at Notre Dame. The first is to learn how to drink. More careers are ruined when people do not know how to hold their alcohol. The second is to learn how to play golf. There is more business done on the golf course than in any boardroom in America. You spend five hours with someone on a golf course and you will get to know him better than five years of calling on him."

The first half of his advice I took to heart. The second part I ignored. If I was going to spend five hours doing something, I was at least going to work up a sweat.

So I didn't learn to play golf until I was in my thirties. What an embarrassment! I have done some things on a golf course that have caused grown people to cry. Not intentionally. I just can't keep from swaying!

When you swing a golf club, you are supposed to be well balanced and you cannot sway.

When I swing a golf club, inevitably I move everything but my bowels!

I wish I was kidding.

Will Rogers characterized golf as "a good walk spoiled." I have felt that way many times.

But I will never forget the first time that I slowed it down and hit a five iron pure and saw the ball draw romantically up toward the sky, curve slightly from right to left and land about 180 yards away. Light bulb!!!!

"Now I get it!" I thought. That was five years after I started playing. I still struggle mightily when I don't play consistently. When I haven't played, I need hours on the range to find that elusive swing. It makes me crazy to watch someone good, who hasn't played in a while, come out to the first tee with no warm-up swings, a bad hangover and still bust it 260 down the middle – then groan, pop open a fresh beer, climb into the golf cart, then express upset at the shot: "I thinned it."

I could smack 'em so hard I could make his head spin. Why can't I do that?

Maybe it's because I have such bad eyes. I really should get LASIK surgery. I don't want to say I have bad eyes, but they are so bad. I basically need a tin cup and a dog.

God forbid I should get them fixed. They say Babe Ruth's eyes were so good that from the batter's box at Yankee Stadium, he could read the license plate of a car parked on the warning track in center field when most couldn't tell what kind of car it was.

I couldn't tell you what kind of car it was if it was parked at second base! But I never thought bad eye sight negatively impacted my golf game. It's all part of the denial process.

I do remember, though, when I thought I had finally nailed it. I brought three of my best customers to Wellesley Country Club. After a wonderful lunch, we headed to the first tee. It was the first time I had ever brought guests, as my golf game was so bad there was a wanted poster of me hanging in the greens keeper's office.

All three of my guests teed off and if you walked out about 240 yards with a blanket, you could have opened it and dropped in the middle of the fairway and it would have covered all three of their balls. I then stepped to the tee, brimming with confidence for the first time I can ever remember on the links.

Now, for some reason, it seemed that every member I knew at that club just happened to be walking by the first tee at that moment. News of my wildly inconsistent play had circulated throughout the club. It had not gone unnoticed to me that people would murmur when I walked by.

I made the mistake of looking around before I addressed the ball.

In times past, anyone who was standing anywhere from nine o'clock to three o'clock was in danger of being hit when I was swinging. But not anymore, I thought. Plus, those guys were only about 240 yards down the fairway. I knew I could fly them with one of my bombs. I'll reach back for a little extra. That was my last swing thought.

And with that picture in my mind, after a couple of waggles, I swung so hard I almost screwed myself into the ground. Oh, and let's not forget the sway. My hips must have changed zip codes I moved them so much.

The result?

The ball came off my open club face and, you guessed it. It screamed about three feet off the ground directly at three o'clock, smashed a golf cart, just missing the pro, ricocheted over to the driving range where it almost decapitated some lady!

I felt like I was in a Southwest Airlines commercial. "Wanna get away?"

A massive groan emanated from the collective mouths of every person there. The pro shook his head and turned away. He had a bewildered member to attend to. I think I also let out a healthy "f-bomb" thereby making my humiliation complete. It got worse after that as I could not get the shot out of my head. The round was one of the worst in my life. I needed a twelve-step program for six months. I was definitely a couple of fries short of a "Happy Meal."

There have been other embarrassing moments. When I was once paired with famous jeweler, Arthur DePrisco, I was so bad that after two holes, I handed my bag to my caddie, instructed him to finish the eighteen and walked off.

One more: When I gathered the nerve to actually enter a tournament, I was pleased that my ten-year-old son, Conor, agreed to caddie for me. His older two brothers knew better. So what did I do? Dropped the old shoulder again, spun around like a top during my swing and, yep, hit another screamer to the right into golf cart. It exploded the Hub-cap and the ball came to a rest some twenty yards BEHIND me!

As my partner shook his head in dismay, my loving son uttered one word: "Pathetic!"

He proceeded to set the bag down and then said, "Sir, you're on your own!"

Not Dad, but Sir! He disowned me right there on the first tee of my own club in front of a gallery! (Conor, who is now a Sergeant in the U.S. Marines, may have given me a second chance and finished the round; I am not sure. It was a "Seinfeld moment" and I have tried to block it all out!)

Golf is also a demonic creation. I have my moments. Being six feet six inches, I can go long when I am swinging the club well but then be horrible the next hole. Two years ago I drove the greens on two 300-plus yard Par 4s on Butch Harmon's home course Rio Secco in Las Vegas. I made an eagle and birdie on both with fellow Keurig employees John Whoriskey, Mike Williamson and David Mattice as witnesses!

But the very next day, I think I shot a buck and a quarter! So sad.

Candidly, I am fairly sure that genes play a very important role in golf. With the disease Huntington's, which killed my mom and both brothers, if you get the gene, you get the disease. It is an inescapable fact.

I think it is the same way with golf. If you have the gene, you are destined to be good at the game. If you don't, I don't care how much you practice, you are going to stink at golf

Jimmy has the gene. I don't. So why do I play?

Because of the camaraderie created by playing with friends and family. It is just the best, and every once in a while I enjoy a break-through, find my swing and play well.

If you are a real golfer, you have to go away on golf trips. There is nothing like a golf trip with friends. Every year, I travel to Pine-hurst North Carolina in early August, to join sixteen other bud-dies, mostly from my high school, St. John's College Prep in Wash-ington, D.C. This year celebrates the twentieth year in Pinehurst for many of the lads.

This year will be my seventh and I am proud to be a part of the "Barrett House Boys:" Freir, Chumper, Rugg, Jorge, Black Jack, Hoggy, the Silver Fox, Hags, Juice, Freddie, Nickie, Bobby McGee, T- Long, Tree, Sparkie, Craig, Richie Bett, the Commish, Blue Burke. Thirty-six holes a day for at least five days. Dinners and drinks together, and so many laughs you need a facial by the end of the week.

But the founder of the Barrett House boys won't be there this year – the man they call "the Knute." Pinehurst is always fun. But with-out Knute, it will never be the same.

I have never played a round of golf with Jimmy but I know how all of Stump's golfing buddies at his club, Creekside Country Club in Salem, are going to feel when Jimmy is gone. I know how Mez, JT, Burskey, Dana, and Steve Viale will miss him. It will be a void which cannot and will not be filled. Jimmy was the heart and soul of any golf group of which he was a member. When you are a member of a golf group, you are part of a brotherhood that is thicker than thieves. Creekside is losing its heart and soul.

The Barrett House boys lost its heart and soul too.

Gary Knutson was so much like Stump. He was mischievous, successful in business, dedicated to his family, and one of greatest all-around athletes I have ever known. Stump had to walk-on to the ND golf team. Knute got a full ride to Kentucky for football.

I remember his acceptance speech at the St. John's Hall of Fame banquet when he was inducted. Brother Timothy Dean was the head disciplinarian at St. John's. When Brother Timothy walked through the halls, we quaked. He was much like the sister portrayed so well by Meryl Streep in the Oscar-nominated film *Doubt*. When you were a student, he was the Prince of Darkness. But after you graduated, he would transform into a wonderful friend.

Knute explained in his speech that he had come back to St. John's during his college years and was eager to share with Brother Timothy that he made the honor roll at Kentucky to which the Christian Brother replied, "Boy, they must be dumb there."

In re-telling the story, Knute turns to Brother Timothy on the dais and deadpans, "Brother, yes they are."

At only five-foot-nine he was an "All Met" in football at St. John's, maybe a better baseball player, a heck of a guard in basketball in his younger years, a swimmer and yes, a single digit handicap in golf. Although when he would arrive for the annual "Tar Hole Cup" outing in August, his handicap would somehow rise and he became known as "Mr. Eleven." His explanations for how his index had risen were always priceless.

Like Stump, he was a money player. Like Stump, he was the life of any party and like Stump, Knute was one of the funniest people I have ever known.

However, there is one big difference between Stump and Knute. Stump is a golf purist. Like my good friend Peter "Hoggy" Grant, you don't mess with the integrity of the game. With Stump and Hoggy, you play them as they lie.

Knute was just the opposite. He could beat just about anyone one on one in golf, following the rules. But in the company of the Barrett House boys, he was Darth Vader, master of the dark side – and we loved it.

One time at Pinehurst, Knute came up to his ball in a tight match. It had landed in what he thought was an unfair rough. Not missing a beat, he reached into his golf bag and pulled out a can of spray paint. He then proceeded to spray paint around the ball on the grass, looked up innocently and proclaimed, "Ground under repair. Free lift!"

Another time he hit his ball into a hazard. Prodded by Freir to play it as it lay, Knute accepted the challenge, took off his shoes and socks and while almost sinking in mud up to his knees he swung at the ball. Knowing Knute, he missed it intentionally. He created a big splash and in one motion on the follow through with his right hand plucked the ball out of the water and threw it up in the air on the green. While Freir roared as he had recorded it, his unsuspecting opponents on the green groaned thinking he had pulled off the impossible as the ball landed feet from the cup.

Too many stories to recount and too many laughs to remember: tracer putts on the greens, fluffing the ball in the rough, banking birdies for later in the match. He was an original. The best image I have of Knute is him driving his golf cart down the railroad tracks with Sparkie in a photo that captures his wonderful mischievous side. I can also hear Hoggy shaking his head repeating his pleas, "Gary, you just can't do that!"

In August 2004, during our week in Pinehurst, he was in my group one day when he just didn't seem like himself. When he got back to the Barrett House, he let Dr. Dave Freitag know he had blood in his stool. Freir did not hesitate to get Knute back to his home in Chapel Hill. Tests ensued and the diagnosis was complete. The indestructible Knute had colon cancer.

Knute did chemo and radiation. He tried everything and battled hard. For a year he did the treatments which tore his body up. The following August he even made it back to Pinehurst to play a few times with the boys. To no one's surprise, he shot lights out the first day at the Governor's Club. Less than three months later, he was gone.

In September that year a couple of weeks before he passed, we gathered at Freir's house to pay tribute to the man they call the Knute. When Knute and I talked before the dinner, he simply said, "Hawk, cancer sucks. I am going to miss you guys."

Jimmy never knew Knute. But the similarities of their lives and of their tragedies is profound to me. If they ever spent a day together they would have become friends for life. Both of them were undersized over-achievers. Both were great athletes. And both Jimmy and Knute were dedicated to their families, their friends and their faith. But neither Knute or Jimmy will enjoy their golden years.

Golf was a big piece of Knute's life. Golf has been a huge part of Jimmy's. Recounting good times with Knute makes me think about Jimmy and how I wished we could have played some golf together. We would have laughed a lot and I probably would be a heck of a lot better golfer than I am today. But I could never become as good a golfer as Stump.

In addition to his Notre Dame achievements, Jimmy has won tournaments just about everywhere he ever played. He was McNary Club champion, Creekside Club champion, and, like Knute, he saved his best for last when he and his frequent playing partner,

Steve Viale, won the two-ball championship at Creekside, two months after Jimmy was diagnosed with ALS.

There will always be a special place in the hearts of everyone Jimmy has ever played a round with. Golf taught Jimmy a lot about life. His passion for the game helped him through tough times when he was a boy, helped him get through Notre Dame and helped give him status in the business world, playing with customers and colleagues. But most of all, it spawned life-long friendships and gave him special time with the love of his life, Melanie.

Jimmy recounted his top ten favorite golf experiences; he has had some great ones.

> *"I would love to recap for you my 10 top golf experiences. I have lived a good life and golf has been a critical part of it so you don't need to feel sorry for me. I hope you enjoy the short versions of stories, especially you golfers. So here goes:*
>
> *1. I always try to do something very special for key dates in my wife Melanie's life. This particular event was her 50th birthday on August 18, 2004. Even though Melanie is not exactly an accomplished golfer she always told me she would like to play one course before she died. On her 50th, we did and it was the best... Pebble Beach Golf Links on the Monterey Peninsula. Even though it was definitely the most expensive round of golf that I ever played it was worth it to see my wife take her clubs off the cart on 18 and walk the 18th fairway. Upon putting out, she was greeted by the pro and presented a medallion bag tag with her name on it... seeing Melanie play Pebble Beach is something I'll cherish forever. As they say – PRICELESS!*

2. Any golfers life's dream is to one day go to the Masters. They call it the "toughest ticket in all of sports". One year my Uncle Leonard Hauprich, brother of my grandmother and best friend "Nana", invited me to go and spend a week with him and his dear wife. We played golf at Orangeburg Country Club, ate, drank and talked non-stop. Then came Thursday. Uncle Len and I were to go to the Masters, just the two of us. We left early and were there when the gates opened. Uncle Len liked two spots: Amen Corner and also around 15, 16, and 7. Uncle Len was a bit older than I was so he liked to stay and sit in those two spots. I wanted to see the whole course and did but always stopped to see how Uncle Len was doing. We had a great lunch together. Ham and cheese or pimento and cheese sandwiches were $2.00 as well as beers in Masters plastic cup souvenir glasses. It doesn't get any better than that. We spent the afternoon together talking and watching the best in the world on the greatest course in the world. It was a beautiful day. It was a dream come true and I have Uncle Len to always thank for that day. Just spending it with him, just the two of us, was as great a day as I'd ever had.

3. When I was transferred from Cincinnati to Portland with Coca-Cola, the parent company, I made an immediate friend with one of the bottler people Chris Burskey in Portland, OR. We both loved golf, shared the same morals and ethics and he seemed like the brother I have never had. For 5 years we planned a trip to Scotland to play the top British Open courses. I'll make this short, but the start of the dream was teeing off on the Old Course at 12 Noon on a beautiful sunny day. I very rarely get nervous on a golf course but I did that day. This was a dream, the home of golf, where it all started and to be there with a buddy was indescribable. The ending couldn't have been scripted better; I hit a big drive, but was a bit long and on the back of the green with the pin up front. It was a little after 4PM and it's a tradition that when the townspeople get off work, they get a pint and circle the 18th green and watch the golfers coming in. As if the golf gods were looking down on me I drained that long putt for a birdie and got a big roar from the townspeople to finish with a 76. Those moments can never be repeated.

4. One of my partners that I played many two-man events with and was quite successful is Tommy Manz. Unfortunately Tommy has developed a type of Parkinson's that has slowed him down a bit but we experienced a round on the links that that not many people have had the pleasure of enjoying. Tommy had a salesman in his company whose dad lived in Monterey on 17 mile drive. Tommy got to talking to the salesman and in a whirl we were invited to play one of the hardest courses to get on in the world, Cypress Point. They have very few members and one member has to accompany each guest. We played a beautiful day and my partner was Mr. Joe Lee, a retired banker from Mellon bank. The course is everything they say it is, the prettiest and most majestic and surreal course I could ever imagine. I had a hot start, 3 under after 5, but the best was when Tommy and I from the back tees on the world famous 16th hole both made par. Again it couldn't have been scripted better; well maybe my birdie on 18 for a 75 to win the match. My partner Mr. Lee, a very wealthy man, looked like he hit the lottery when we won the match... and won a quarter!

5. The Tournament Players Championship has become what a lot of people call the 5th major. (Not me) People forget that after the pros played there the first year they swore they would never come back again; it was too tough. My buddy, Chris Burskey, and I planned a trip to play this course that was so tough. As usual we played from the tips (all the way back where the pros play.) Needless to say it is a much different course today than it was then. Talk about tough! No wonder the pros complained as many couldn't break 80. One of my favorite golf stories ever was when Chris (a 12-14 handicap) birdied the 16th hole, which back then NOBODY could hit in two; he parred the 17th, the island hole; hooked his drive into the water on 18 and made a great double bogey. Tally it up, 1 over for the last three holes on one of the toughest courses around. Now what did he shoot for the course? A SMOOTH 118!

6. Melanie and I had always wanted to take a vacation to Sydney, Australia. It takes a lot of planning as it's so far away so you might as well go for a period of time. After we sold our stores and saved up for 5 years we rented an apartment in Sydney and spent a month there. That's the way to do it, live with the locals; it was an experience of a lifetime. We played a lot of golf but the capper was playing New South Wales. They treated us like a king and queen. They gave me a locker adjacent to those of three pretty good Aussies… Greg Norman, Steve Elkington and Robert Allenby, then me. Pretty good company! The course is as scenic a course as I've ever played and that includes Pebble Beach that I've played many times. It was our favorite trip and to play that course was an experience we'll never forget.

7. When my Coca-Cola buddy, Chris Burskey and I were in Scotland, we got the bright idea that since we were there, we HAD to go see THEE Open. The problem was we were staying at the Marine Highland Hotel next to Troon Golf Course and THEE Open was at Muirfield which is on the complete other side of the country. No problem. We left around 3AM and drove across country, (if you've ever been to Scotland you can imagine the drive we had; no highways; all two maybe one and a half lane roads). Well we made it as the gates opened and watched for about 4 hours, and got back in the car to drive back across the country back to the Troon area. Why you ask? We had a 4:30 tee time at Prestwick, one of the oldest clubs in Scotland; used to be part of THEE Open rotation. We made the time, barely. After 14 holes it didn't just start raining, it was like a hurricane. You know when to quit when your bag fills up with water! (No carts there, you tote your clubs) What's worse is the clubhouse is for members only. Well these members saw us trudging in looking like soaked rats and invited us into the men's bar. They have tankards on the wall with their names on them. They bought us as many beers as we could consume and said we were more like the Scottish than Americans. That's the ultimate compliment from a Scotsman!

8. On the same trip we played the hardest course I have ever to this day played and under tough very windy conditions; Carnoustie – commonly referred to as Car-Nastie. I've had some pretty low rounds in my career but this was by far the best considering the course, playing where the pros play and under very windy conditions. 75 might not sound great, but believe me it's the best round I've ever played… period!

9. The first Peter Jacobsen tournament for charities was held at Portland Golf Club, (A Ryder Cup was held there one year.) Coca-Cola was a major sponsor and this was the first tournament Peter had ever put on. He knew I had met Mr. Arnold Palmer before so he wanted me to caddie for him. He asked us if we would help him in the beverage areas and also help with any marketing ideas we might be able to come up with to raise more money. Peter is about the most likeable guy you'd ever want to meet. My boss who was president, while I was Director of

Sales, kind of gave me leeway to help Peter in any way I could. I'll never forget the day Peter came into my office and said, "Jim, we have a problem." The problem was he had sold all the caddie uniforms to different companies. No problem there, but the companies used them as sales contests, incentives, etc. and the problem was none of the caddies knew much about golf. I said, "You're right Peter that IS a problem." We're talking Greg Norman, Freddie Couples, Fuzzy Zoeller, Gary Player, Curtis Strange, Tom Watson, Peter and Arnie, not exactly slouches! Luckily I had played quite a few rounds at Portland. I had even taken my wife out to help me get yardages some early evenings. I knew the course. So I told Peter to put Mr. Palmer and me in the first group each of the two days. I left little notes around the course with yardages on them for the groups behind us. As a result, some very inexperienced caddies were able to provide yardage distances they never would have known. It turned out great. The tournament was a grand success for many years. I remember feeling like I lost 30 pounds in 2 days working my butt off, but it was worth it!

10. In no particular order, the following are tied for tenth. The rounds I have played the most with, Rich Mesnick, my first boss out of college and one of my best friends after 32 years of hanging around together. The rounds in Palm Springs, Hillcrest, Rancho Park and so many others... Royal County Down, Portmarnock and Ballybunion in Ireland, Troon and North Berwick in Scotland. Riviera in LA. My 64 course record at Notre Dame and on another occasion a 274 (-18) Notre Dame Open record. The many two-man tournaments another buddy, Steve Viale and I have won over the years. Between him and Tommy Manz, I've been blessed to have the two best tournament partners you can imagine with complementary games. My 12:30 Friday afternoon group games... a book could be written on just these; Steve Viale, Peter Juhren, Dr. Monte Morgan and the one and only Steve "Reno" Rentfro. My 64 from the blue tees at Creekside, my home course. Gosh there are so many memories. All the wonderful people I've met on the golf course where you really learn about a person... and so many of these people have been so generous to ALS and my fundraising efforts... I am such a lucky man."

Jimmy has enjoyed so many golf experiences – so many tournament wins, so many spectacular golf courses with so many good friends. But his trip with his Coke buddy Chris Burskey may have topped them all.

I met Chris Burskey one hot day in Phoenix. All I could think of was how special a golf friendship can be and what an amazing friend Jimmy is to those he loves.

Chris Burskey and the Old Sod

Jimmy arrived in Oregon in 1982. After doing a great job in his initial Coke capacity, Jimmy did an amazing job as the Diet Coke Introductory Coordinator. He had developed some great friends along the way, but none would become closer to him than a fellow Coke manager in Portland, Chris Burskey.

Jimmy had been promoted to the position of director of sales for Coca-Cola Bottling of Oregon. Chris Burskey was one of his colleagues. Jimmy was now really in a coaching role. His mission was to inspire the bottlers to increase sales and distribution for Coke products at a rate much higher than that created by his predecessor.

This new position also afforded Jimmy the chance to play a lot of customer golf. During his first year in Oregon, Jimmy was still the mischievous bachelor. It would not be until 1983 that he would marry the lovely Melanie. During that initial year, he sold a lot of Coke, played a lot of golf and partied often, mostly with his new friend Burskey.

Chris Burskey met me at a great local restaurant just outside of Phoenix. We didn't have much time and we had never met before. Jimmy had told me a bit about his burly buddy but, with Burskey, seeing is believing. The Arizona climate and Burskey's skin are a match made in heaven. "El Sol" loves to beat down on the backs of Arizona residents and Burskey welcomes it with open arms. Even George Hamilton would be envious of Burskey's tan.

Burskey is now retired. He and Jimmy went back to the Coca-Cola days from 1979 to 1987. He now spends his time helping out his aging mom and occasionally ventures out for a golf outing.

An avid golfer, the "Bursk" and Jimmy played a lot of golf. One of their dreams was to go over the big pond to Scotland and play some of the famous Scottish courses right around the time of the British Open. Back in the early 1990s, "Bursk" was about a ten handicap and Jimmy was about a two. After years of talking about planning a trip, Jimmy finally made it happen and he planned the whole thing.

As Chris and I finished lunch and settled into a comfort zone of communication at the restaurant, the cherubic Burskey opened up about his long-time friend Jimmy and their golf trip to Scotland.

"I have just never met anyone like him. He really is an amazing man with extraordinary amounts of determination," he said, his voice starting to quiver. "We have been through so much together. He was an amazing salesman, a great friend, and a money golfer. He planned everything as he always does right down to the last detail. All I had to do was show up and not mess up my flight arrangements.

"I remember our trip to Scotland in 1992 like it was yesterday. Jimmy arranged the whole thing. The trip was just one of the greatest experiences of my life. At the end, I thought I wish I had kept a diary. Then, a few days after I returned home, this came in the mail for me." Now his voice was more than quivering.

With his face flushed with pride, Burskey handed over a small green, personally embossed hardcover notebook. On the cover it read, "Bursk House – Scotland 1992."

I opened it and flipped through it. It was filled with wonderful photos as well as a blow by blow accounting of the trip written from Jim's perspective, clearly for his good friend. I didn't have time to read it there in front of Chris, and it would have assuredly embarrassed him to do so. But it is perfectly typed on a regular old typewriter and it contains details few guys would bother remembering. Chris indicated that whenever he reads it, which he often does, it is so easy to flash back to sixteen years ago and live the trip all over again.

To give you an idea of the kind of guy Jimmy is, and what his friends mean to him, I read the whole thing and felt as if I had lived their dream as well. It is written by Jimmy. If you are a golfer who has ever enjoyed this kind of golf trip structured around the British Open, this is a treat. If you are not a golfer, bear with me. Try to look at this as further evidence of how special Jimmy is to do this for a very close friend.

7/11/92

Left house at 7:20 arriving at airport about 1 hour later. Said good bye to Mel, boarded a United flight at 9:20 AM., leaving at 9:50. Read a lot, had some sort of rubbery chicken, good pasta, a salad, rye bread, a couple of Cokes and two cookies. (Walkers Rich Biscuits- shortbread) from Aberlou, Scotland- how ironic. Had an article in Flight Mag. on Scotland's Single Malt Heritage. I hate scotch but Burskey says I've got to try it- it's different. We'll see. The article says Royal Lochnagar Reserve is the elite of the elite as Queen Victoria gave it her seal of approval as the official distiller to the Queen. They only produce 3,000 btls./yr.. It costs $165 a bottle.

Watched 3ʳᵈ rnd. of the Sr. Open, had a beer and was the only person of 25 people that spoke English except the bartender who also spoke Spanish. This is the Chicago airport!

Boarded British Airways plane at 3:10 PDX time, 5:10 Chi. time and departed at 5:47, the last time on Amer. soil for a week. It's supposed to be a 6 hr. 45 min. flight and the time diff. is 6 hrs- Chi. and 8 hours PDX. Was presented with some juice, a menu and Burskey arrived at 3:05; had engine trouble in Atl. All his baggage came in, mine to come in at 3:30. Made friends with a cop, and "BSe"d with him and David- 3:30- no bags on flight-they'll look into it and get them to St. Andrews tonight

Drove to St .Andrews- only one wrong turn, Burskey likes left shoulder. Countryside looks like Oregon. Crossed a mammoth bridge heading north {then he has the #1 and #2 circled, indicating which pictures to look at when he describes something in writing... Jimmy gives a whole new meaning to the word "organization"}.

After crossing Burskey tried to put his seat belt on and got stopped by the cops for swerving. "Are you on holiday?" Were you looking at a map?" "I see... take a breath test". No problem- a warning-"Have a great holiday".

Continued on to St. Andrews (3,4,5,6,7,8) Took picture of Burskey with Firth behind him (9). Got to hotel at about 6:30. Our group already invited to a cocktail party.

We showered, shaved, had a beer and joined them for dinner. Excellent tomato bisque soup, duck and tangerine salad with asparagus spears, fantastic monkfish, w/a light wine sauce, and an excellent array of vegetables. Glass of wine followed by Rasp. and cream for Bursk and an ice cream vanilla and bramble in a cup with 2 sauces just like in Paris. If the meals are like this, it'll be heaven. Had coffee and headed out.

Drove to the R&A (Royal St. Andrews course). *Took picture of both of us in front. (9,10, 11) Walked the 17th and 18th- absolutely unbelievable. The greens are humongous and undulated beyond belief. St. Andrews golf shop (12) is very tiny. The St. Andrews Woolen Mill and Tom Morris Gold Shop (13) very expensive. Forget cashmere (500-1400 per sweater).*

St. Andrews Men's Clubhouse is down from Tom Morris (14). Champions bar, the ultimate 19th hole; (15, 16) and some long views from the 18th tee (17, 18). The most unbelievable sight is the R&A lit up at night (19, 20, 21). Had a beer at Chariots Bar with Muriel, the bartender (Chariots of Fire crew stayed there). Met a guy from Oslo on holiday by himself for 10 days, 4 rounds at the Old Course and 3 at the New. Says New is tougher. Further discussion – this led to his 28 handicap! Burskey had a 12 year old single Malt – I tried – yech! Made it back to the hotel at 11:45, talked to BA about the luggage- still nothing new and took about 30 sec. to fall asleep.

Mon. 7/13/92

Got up 7:30, great sleep- sorely needed. Nice room overlooking beautiful gardens, Nicklaus stays here. Juice, cereal, eggs, what they call bacon, fruit, coffee. Drove into town, went to 4-5 shops. Beautiful sweaters - average price $100. Found out if I need I can rent clubs for 6 pounds. Went back to hotel- and the first sign of the golfing gods- my clubs have arrived!! Changed clothes (a real welcome) and drove to the old course- where the great game began. Putted on the practice green, rented trolleys, and promptly teed off at 12:12. Burskey and I hit *great drives right down the middle. Both of us were short of breath teeing off as emotions took over. After all these years talking about it we're finally doing it. It's hard to believe. It's pretty open but if you get in the deep rough it's real, real tough. The pothole bunkers (22) are the real problem. It's mostly luck, or unlucky I should say, but if you get in one you just have to wedge it out.*

Burskey still has that classic swing – Rock, waggle, fart, spit, and bombs away... great follow through (23). The shots of the day were as follows: #9 CB short drive, blasts out of trap shanking it into caddie's bag (will become part of St. Andrews lore according to the caddie who has caddied 11 years and has never seen anything like it. Same hole, I drove it 300+ yards but into left bunker at the green. Had a 45 yard sand shot, blasted 10 feet passed and it sucked back to a foot for a tap-in birdie.

On #17, the famous "Road Hole" (24), Caddie said aim for "O" in "Old". I hit it great right of the O but not high enough, hit shed, but the golfing gods came through again as it ricochets about 220 yards down the middle of fairway; Caddie gave me a quick lesson on how to get out of Hell Bunker after I busted a 3-wood but hit it right into the bunker the pros say is the worst. Regular club face 1/2" behind the ball and it amazingly pops right out, defying the laws of physics.

To the 18th (25, 26, 27). This has to be the greatest sight for a golf historian in the world. The R&A, the village, the people, the Open, the start of golf. I creamed a drive over the road and had only a sand wedge left. The locals, after finishing work, have lined the green and the right side of the fairway. I hit it to 20 ft. but past the hole with about a 3 ft left to right downhill breaking putt. Thank you golfing gods; right in the center and a great applause from the gallery- I can assure you I'll never forget this feeling for the rest of my life.

Next stop the Niblick Tavern where the caddies and the pros when they are here (especially Woosie) hang out. Had a few pints with our caddies, Alex Barr who Burskey gave a hat to and Alex McMullan who offered a bedroom in his house for the '95 Open (28).

Next- the Homelea Hotel down the street. Met the owner, Don Sutherland (29) and he offered his bed and breakfast to us at 20 pounds a person per night. We hear that when the Open is played here the prices are staggering. Next stop Chariots bar with a quickie with Muriel before going back the hotel for dinner.

I went up to call Maurice- Burskey ordered for both of us. Had East Coast Seafood Chowder- unbelievably good. Lamb ragu for CB, Beef for me. Rasp & Cream for CB and choc. truffle for me. A long eventful day- very emotional; went to bed a little after 11.

Tues. 7/14/92

Same breakfast. Went to bank, made Norma's day. Bought postcards and stamps. Teed off at St. Andrews New Course at 10:30 (31). No trolleys, had to hump the bags. Tougher, more challenging than the Old; more character. After round, had fish and chips. Chris had 4 Cokes, me 3 and 3 pints of water, both seriously thirsty and Burskey's dogs are yelping! Teed off the old course at 4:40, winning a very lucky lottery for an extra tee time. Burskey promptly birdied the first hole while the wheels came off for me. In pot bunker, and then blast over green to firth. Pick up Bursk, next hole! #17 I cleared the shed this time, no paint. Bursk made putt of the day on #18 for par. We're beat. Time for Niblick!.

Beers/dinner with the boys. Met golf tour operator and a wonderful chap from Glasgow, a engineer who is a member of St. Andrews. Invited us as guests to the Open in '95 – Tempting – Met 4 "laimes" from South England that just got back from the Open at Muirfield. They invited us to St. Anne's next year. One took Couples and gave me the field. Golf tour operator wanted to bet Burskey Colin Montgomery would finish better than Nick Faldo. We could make some money. Faldo won and Couples and "Montie" didn't even make the cut. Another gas of a guy was Ian, a caddie whose mother is Polish. He bought sweater for me for 20 pounds. Great deal. Took last pictures of the R&A. Drove slowly home and hit the sack at midnight.

Wed. 7/15/92

Slept til 8, had breakfast and checked out. Went to town and bought sweaters for Mom and Dad and a sweatshirt for Shawn. Burskey bought 2 prints and I got shirt at Old Tom Morris' Shop. Drove to Carbnoustie (NE), got a little hung up in CB's new favorite city, Dundee. He loves "roundabouts", the left lane and the white line; Carnoustie was spectacular – great layout, exceptional architecture and as we've heard in unexpectedly great shape (34, 35, 36, 37). Famous bunkers (38), Johnny Miller's hole (39). Burskey in the crap again (40). I made a ton of putts, shot 75, had three sandies and 2 doubles from impossible areas. Both of us birdied 11, a very unlikely occurrence. I birdied 17 with a 60 footer, and parred 18 hitting a 5 wood (230) 8 feet past and lipped it out coming back. Last three holes as tough as it gets. Saw Caledonia Golf Club (41) and then went to Clubhouse and had a beer

*with members (42). Got some Cokes, took a last picture
and started the long drive to Troon*

*Got screwed up in Perth, stopped at a Safeway Superstore,
as nice as any in the US. Bought ham, salami, cheese,
bread, chips (salt and vinegar- CB's love) and apples.
Continued on and stopped off at Gleaneagles, one of
Lifestyles of the Rich and Famous Top Ten. Posh, over
$400 a night (45, 46, 47, 48, 49). Tried to have a beer-
no deal- have to have coat and tie. Continued on to Troon,
arriving at 9:15 (CB 7 miles from Troon hits gravel left of
white line, swerving perfectly back onto road). Got semi-
settled and went down to dinner after taking CB's picture
in front of our hotel, Marine Highland (50). Fruit and
sorbet for me, pate and soup for Burskey. Both had good
sole and I had apple tart w/cinnamon ice cream. Burskey
had lemon soufflé and we both had two pints of Scotland's
finest. Chit-chatted with group and a husband and wife
that Chris met on the plane flight from Atlanta. Hit the
sack at midnight thinking of Troon.*

Thurs. 7/16/92

*Got up early at 6:30, did postcards and left for Troon.
Called Rufflets in St. Andrews to retrieve Burskey's travel
bag that he forgot. Burskey got car from lot, pulled it
around front only to find out we had 500 yard walk to
the Clubhouse. Met the caddie master and starter, paid
our $130 and went into the bar to have bad coffee and
cookies. Met up with some guys from Orlando, Jim and
Phil and teed off in the rain and wind at 9:40. This is a
true "linkside" monster! (51, 52). Beautifully contoured
along the lay of the land. Memorable shots: #6 JC 40 footer
for birdie; #8 Postage Stamp- Burskey hits a 7 iron 10 feet
from the pin. (53)... a very nice $160 shot! JC on the
same hole hits great sand shot to 4 feet from left trap (54,*

*55). #11- JC 481 yd. par 4- hit 4 iron 15 feet for par (56)-
#15 JC hit pin with chip. #16 CB sandie. Took pictures of
guys walking up 17th tee with our hotel in the background
(57, 58). #17 CB holed sand shot for birdie.*

*Took pictures of #18 (59, 60). CB finished par-birdie-
bogey; JC 38 back nine for 80. This is one great golf course,
extremely tough. Par 4s 438-481-431-465-457-452,, 542
par 5 and a 223 par 3. When we finished, we thanked
the caddie master and starter. Had lunch, which was
included, CB corned beef and soup, JC a "steakwich",
and a shrimp sandwich and the customary two pints of
lager. Decided to take it easy as our legs were tired and
our feet hurt. Watched the British Open. Burskey took
a nap and I took a steam, whirlpool and shower. Very
refreshing. Had a couple of pints before dinner and
listened to our "wonderful" L.A. friends Bert and Mark
tell us how tough the course they played on and how easy
they heard Troon was. Troon is as tough a course as I
have ever played. These two are becoming real tough to
take. Capped the night off with a nice glass of port after a
nice dinner- CB- salmon, little dry and a lemon cheesecake
with rasp. essence; JC- beef stew (not as good as CB's)-
apricot biscuit with apricot ice cream. Hit the sack early
as wake up call is 3:00 AM for THEEEE Open!*

Fri. 7/17/92

*Rose at 3:30- Geez it's early. Jackie secured us a couple
of Cokes (I won't tell Burskey they are Pepsis!)- at this
hour we should get dispensation. Left for Muirfield at
4:40. THEE Open (61). 16 pounds to enter- 5 pounds to
park. America should take note of what the Scots do for
a tournament. Not much traffic. We lucked out as people
said it would take us 3- 3 ½ hours. It took us only 2 hours
and 10 minutes. Huge stands with seats on 12 of the 18*

holes. Very comfortable and great viewing. Followed Floyd, Kite and Price for 10 holes and then Weiskopf and Player to see the rest. Pate and Floyd are -7 after the first round. Orrin Vincent !!! is -4- quite impressive. Cook was -5 for 11 holes- -9 total seems to be making a move. Darran Lee the only amateur to make the cut. Donnie Hammond -7 as is Ernie Els from South Africa. Faldo unbelievable 64 including eagle. Tough wind- tied lowest round in history, lowest 36 holes in history. Nicklaus, Watson, Couples, Montgomerie, Seve all missed the cut. Faldo -12, Cook and Brand -9, Pate -8. Course doesn't seem that tough.

Tents are unbelievable if you have a lot of money. Bought Mel gorgeous sweater map of Scotland with all the Open venues. CB bought two more prints and now has all the courses we played. Has spent about $300 and it will take at least that to frame them, but they are nice. He's going to need a larger house and office. Took some more very illegal picture on the way out coming down the 18th fairway (63, 64, 65). Left for Prestwick near Troon at noon.

Arrived at 3:00, wore shorts all day. CB birdied #1 (66). JC birdied 10 with an 8 iron from 173. Yes the wind is picking up (68). The #4 hole is an unbelievable blind par 3, 213 yards. JC hit the green but the story is our "good pal" Bert. Hit it up against left bunker under lip. Tried to hit it left handed. WHIFFED. Swung again – STILL IN BUNKER. Hit again- FELL BACKWARDS SPREAD EAGLED INTO TRAP. What a sight. Instructed caddie (Gary) to help him out. One of the clubs slipped and NAILED BERT IN THE FOREHEAD. PERFECT – Even broke skin.

The wind is really howling and it looks ugly. One par 3 on back side CB hit perfect 3 wood on 185 yard hole- 45 yards short. JC hit perfect 5 wood 30 yards short. CB nice blast on #13 (69). With a 6 iron and JC an 8 iron 165 yards- both within 10 feet. Then the weather. Hurricane winds, heavy, heavy rain- time to call it a day.

Met great guy names Martin Shore from Pelshie in the club house, a real character. Had 2 pints with members and their "tankards". Drive back to Marine Highland, about 5 minutes, thank goodness. We cleaned out the car, had a pint, showered, met the group in a bar before going to dinner. Fish again, dessert so-so, couldn't last forever. Took a group picture (70). Burskey made the rounds of saying good byes (71) and we hit the hay at 11:00.

Sat. 7/18/92

Wake up call at 5:00. Showered, packed and on the road to Glasgow airport. Stopped for gas, Cokes and a few more of Burskey's vinegar chips. Lengthy check-in... got screwed up on VAT tax, had a beer and boarded plane at 10:20, taking off at 10:50. Braised beef so-so and free Bailey's with coffee. On to Chicago. Can you believe it? They lost my luggage again. Incredible. Made connections with 5 minutes to spare after filling out paperwork. On to Portland, the last leg. Beef medallions, so-so, bad salad, very good apple crisp. Got in at 6:00 and got Mel's message as to location of van (she left for LA this morning). I loaded up... 92 degrees, paid my $18 for parking and on to Salem.

Stopped off at office and called Mel in L.A. and got home about 8:30. Talked to Dorothy (Mother-in-law) for a couple of hours and fell fast asleep after a long, long day, but with memories of a life long dream trip!

Sun 7/19/92

I know diary should have ended yesterday but after taking Dorothy to airport, Burskey called about 10:45 or 12:45 St. Louis time. He just got in!!! He missed his connection in London, had to stay overnight in Atlanta after thinking he had to spend the night in Cincy. He can look forward to flying again tomorrow morning. Maybe

Other Passengers on Tour & Descriptions
The Yolton gang- Guy, Guy Jr., David & Thomas.
Strange group. Didn't play two days. One used to be a stand-up comedian- I think he took too many drugs
John Merriman & Barbara Beatty- Chris thinks they're married. I don't. John's a drip; Barbara's ok.... From Des Moines Iowa.
Jim and Lana Walker from Huntington Beach Cal- Nice couple
Judy and Joel Widelitz from Seal Beach Ca.- Also nice couple who played with the Walkers. Ladies sat out a couple of rounds.
Don LeClaire & Ira Odle from Indianapolis- Played with John and Barbara usually
And last but not certainly least... Burt Morrow and son Mark. Played 5 rounds with these jerks. Mark's a 7; hits it a ton but is erratic as hell. House would bet the ranch against him in an even up game. Both argue about everything. They also think they're right about everything. Had enough of Mark's "let's play a real golf course". The final picture (72) says it all. Ole Doc is still arguing with Burskey as Burskey is politely telling him to stick it where the sun don't shine!

Epilogue

Best Course- St. Andrews Old- the history makes it
Best Architecture- Carnoustie
Toughest- Troon
Most Memorable Shots- House (Jim) birdies #18 at St. A
Old and receives ovation from townspeople and Burskey
holes sand shot at #17 on Troon
Worst Shot- Burskey shanked sand shot into caddie's bag
out of trap on #9 at St. A Old
Worst Muffed Shot(s)- Burskey's 4 shots from pot
bunkers at #11 St. A Old (and then into the Firth!)
Best Carom Shot- House off the shed at the Road Hole
(caromed 220 yards in the middle of the fairway)
Best Caddie- Alex Bain St. Andrews
Best Pub- Niblick
Best Bartender- Muriel at Champions Bar
Best Beer- Casetlmaine XXX
Best Hotel- Marine Highland, Troon
Best Seafood- Seafood Stew Rufflets Hotel- St. Andrews
Best Sight- #17 Fairway St. A looking down #18
Most Hospitable- Scot- John Henderson- St. Andrews
Best/Worst Cops- The Bridge duo over the Firth
Worst Prediction- (tie) "Couple will win the Open" and
"Montgomerie will finish higher than Faldo"
Worst Driving City- "Dundee"
Worst Driving Obstacle- "Roundabouts"
Best Part of Trip- Living out a dream with your best
buddy!!!!

Burskey later sent me an e-mail and retold some fun stories of his good friend, Jimmy. He just wishes he had one more chance to tee it up with the most special guy he has ever met.

In Burskey's own words:

The First Meeting

It was near the end of my first year working for Coca-Cola in Portland, Oregon in December of '82 when one day a short cocky guy wearing a suit walked in to our offices in the NW Industrial District on Yeon Ave.

"Hi, my name is Jim Culveyhouse, I am the new SDM for Coca-Cola USA. I just moved here from Cincinnati, Ohio."

I was the Advertising and Sales Promotion Manager for the local Coke Bottler in the Portland area. I also had sales call responsibility for several convenience store and drug store customers for the Bottler. As a result of these two jobs, I would have a great deal of contact with the new SDM. So it was great that he and I seemed to "hit it off" right from the start. After a long day of meetings and "getting to know the people and the market conditions," Jim offered to buy me a beer after work.

Little did either of us know that this was the beginning of a long, liquid filled, golf related and mutual interest related friendship. I suggested that we go the Goose Hollow Inn. This eclectic tavern served beer, some wine and the best Ruben sandwiches west of New York. It was owned by Bud Clark who later gained fame as the man in the rain coat flashing a statue in Downtown Portland headlined "Expose Yourself to Art". That fame propelled him to be the mayor of Portland. One beer led to two which led to several pitchers of beer followed by Ruben sandwiches, pizza and more beer.

We started at 6:30 PM. At 12:30 AM the owners swept us out of the tavern with the trash. The entire evening cost less than $30.00 and was the beginning of a friendship *which has lasted from that day until today – some twenty-six years.*

In that time Jimmy helped me through two divorces, two major job changes, several near job firings, retirement and many other problems. There were many times when we would not see each other for several years. But we always remained in contact and whenever we did get together, it seemed like the gap in time was only days and not years

He has helped me build a deck, sell a car, learn how to make business presentations, deal with the stock market, invest money, get rid of bad romantic relationships and plan great golf trips.

The First Thanksgiving

By the fall of 1983 Jimmy and I were fast friends. We worked together, played golf together, drank frequently together and with our wives (Jean Burskey and Melanie Culveyhouse) we socialized together.

For years I have hated turkey. One of the best Thanksgivings I ever had was spent in New England during my time with Ringling Bros. Circus. My wife's family came to visit us in Springfield, Mass. We traveled to Plymouth, Mass. to see the Mayflower and the Pilgrim's village. During that visit we ate lobster for Thanksgiving. I also developed a taste for steamer clams, New England clam chowder and other New England dishes during the three months I was promoting the Circus in Springfield.

At thanksgiving of 1983, I decided that I would become a contrarian and NOT eat turkey for Thanksgiving. I proposed that we buy shrimp, clams and lobsters and make a New England thanksgiving dinner.

We invited Jim and Melanie Culveyhouse to join us for the day. We told them what the menu was (shrimp cocktails, clam chowder, corn on the cob, boiled new potatoes and steamed Maine lobster followed by pumpkin pie for desert) and asked them to bring the beer.

We started the day in the late morning with NFL football, beer and snacks. The afternoon progressed with more beer and food with the addition of Uker (a Midwestern card game)

Finally, we got around to the main course of lobster, corn and potatoes followed by more beer and more card playing. The card game was the guys versus the girls. It featured verbal abuse, yelling in celebration of victory and jibes between the sexes of failure and superiority. The final result of the card game was 25 games for the guys and 1 victory for the girls.

After about 14 hours of memorable fun and too much beer and food the 1st New England Thanksgiving Dinner went into the books as a great success. To this day that experience is still talked about and cherished as "the best Thanksgiving ever"

The First Golf Trip

During the late spring of 1984 I got the hair-brained scheme of putting together a promotion for Coke involving the Portland Oregonian (the major metropolitan daily newspaper in Portland). It involved getting an airline and a hotel chain in Florida to offer consumers the opportunity to win trips to Florida during the winter.

Since it starts raining in Oregon in late September and doesn't quit until the following June, I felt that the offer of a Florida vacation would be well received and would create more sales for Coke products in the Oregon market.

In addition to getting all the prize trips for the promotion, I was able to get a free trip for me. Since my then-wife and I were about to get a divorce, I needed and wanted to get the heck away from her for a while and enjoy myself in Florida. I told Jimmy about the trip and we came up with the idea of getting together in Florida to play golf at the new course in the Jacksonville area called TPC Sawgrass – the famous course with the island green on the Parr 3 17ᵗʰ hole. Thus was born the infamous First Golf Trip.

I flew to Florida and spent six days in the Tampa area relaxing and getting away from work and concerns about my marriage. I then drove up to Jacksonville on a Friday to pick Jimmy up from the airport to start our little golf holiday.

Typically, the plane was late getting in and also typically, Jimmy was in the mood for some drinks. We stopped at a large liquor store on the way to the golf course to "stock-up" for the weekend. After spending over $50.00 on beer and vodka, we proceeded to Sawgrass to check into the hotel and make it to the golf course for the first round.

After the round of golf, we stopped in the clubhouse for drinks and secure recommendations on local "hot spots." It all went downhill from golf. We ended up getting lost, getting into a pool shooting contest and almost a fight; we got thrown out of one restaurant because Jimmy tried to play waiter and ended up trying his famous champagne "trickling down trick" where he stacks glasses, one on top, 6 on the bottom and fills up the top one and lets it trickle down and fill all the glasses. I've seen him do this successfully many times. Problem one – this time no champagne, just red burgundy wine, but that didn't stop Jimmy. He still tried it and proceeded to spill a glass of burgundy wine on a female patron's white dress. "Outta here!"

The last day of the trip featured a round of golf at the most difficult course either of us had ever played. We then ate alligator at a local restaurant and got invited by the owner to stay after closing to drink and eat oysters with him and his restaurant staff.

Our favorite memory during the round of golf at TPC Sawgrass, occurred while standing on the first tee, looking out toward the fairway in the early morning mist. We both turned to each other at the same time and said, "Where the hell do you hit the ball?" When people ask me what I shot that day I say, "I birdied #16, had a par on number 17 and double bogeyed number 18 after hitting in the water." They say there are no good double bogeys but this was one of the all time best, to shoot 1 over for the last 3 holes. I then have to tell them that I shot a 118 for the entire round.

We still have the score cards and the pictures from that trip. Remember this was after the first year the pros played the course and said it too difficult and would never play their again. Now, after many revisions, it's the home of the Players Club Championship

The Hot Dog Stories

If there is anyone who loves hot dogs more than me it is Jim Culveyhouse. There is something special about a hot dog that brings to mind baseball games, rounds of golf and just simple mouth-watering enjoyment.

Jimmy and I experienced the agony and the ecstasy of hot dogs while living and working in Oregon.

Jimmy lived in Vancouver, Washington, when he first moved to the Portland area. Like most Coca-Cola USA employees sent to the Oregon market to work, he purchased a house in Washington to avoid living in Oregon and paying the high Oregon income taxes. Washington had a sales tax but no income tax. Oregon had no sales tax but a high income tax. By living in Washington, Jimmy could avoid the Oregon income tax while buying all of this clothes, food, and furniture in Oregon to avoid the Washington sales tax.

Since Jimmy loved hot dogs and had some free time while working he began a search for the best place to buy and eat hot dogs. After several months of living in Vancouver, Jimmy discovered this man who had a New York City type hot dog stand in downtown Vancouver. This guy had everything to put on a hot dog that you could imagine. You could get anything from a plain dog to a New York style dog (mustard, onions and sour kraut) to a Chicago style dog (celery salt, tomato relish, mustard and a hot pepper). This place was hot dog heaven.

We discovered the "agony" of hot dogs in Eugene, Oregon, at Autzen Stadium during a football game between the Fighting Ducks of Oregon and the Cougars of Washington State University.

That game was one of the best college football games I have ever attended. The score was something like 46 to 42. A running back for Washington St. ran for over 300 yards. It was like neither team had a defense. The weather went from rain to snow to sunshine. We brought a thermos of hot coffee spiked with whisky to keep warm and planned on buying some hot dogs to eat during the game.

Little did we know that it would have been better for us to have eaten the money instead of trying to eat the hot dogs.

It seems like Autzen Stadium was trying to save money and claim that they were offering a higher quality turkey dog for their customers. The claim was that this dog was better for you than the regular pork stuffed hot dog available everywhere else.

Well, during half time, Culveyhouse and I went up to the concession stand and purchased two hot dogs each. We loaded them up with our favorite toppings and headed back to our seats. Once we got seated, we opened up the paper on the dogs and each took a large bite. After one chew and no more that 4 seconds later, we turned to each other with a look of disgust on our faces. We than spit out our mouthfuls of hot dog and threw the dogs in the trash.

I don't think either of us has been in Autzen Stadium since.

Burskey then recounted his feelings earlier described in detail about the golf trip to Scotland Jimmy organized.

The Trip Present

Jim Culveyhouse is always unpredictable. Just when you think you may have him figured out; he will surprise you. Let me tell you about two of Jim's surprises.

In July, 1992 Jim and I went to Scotland for a week. I left St. Louis and arrived in Glasgow (about 4-5 hours late) via Atlanta and London's Gatwick airport. Jim left Portland and while he arrived on time, his airline managed to lose his golf clubs. As you can well imagine, it is difficult to play golf without your golf clubs.

Somehow, everything worked out OK. Jim's clubs were delivered to the hotel several hours before we were set to tee-off at the Old Course at St. Andrews.

But, I digress from my main story. The first surprise from Jim arrived before dinner the first night we were in Scotland.

Jim is a picky eater. In fact, his favorite meal of ALL time consists of the following:

> *Mrs. Paul's fish sticks*
> *Stouffers macaroni & cheese*
> *Or' Ida French fries*
> *Radishes*
> *Green Onions*
> *Some type of cheap beer or Coke*

MUCH to my surprise, at dinner that evening while we were looking at the menu, Jim turned to me and said, "Why don't you order dinner for me?"

I could have been knocked off my chair by the slight waving of a very small bird feather. Not only did I order dinner for Jim that night, but I ordered every meal for him for the entire trip. Even more surprising than him letting me order for him was the fact that he liked what I ordered and ate everything with great enjoyment.

Who said that a leopard can't change his spots? But the BIG surprise was to come later.

About 3-4 weeks after I returned from our trip of a lifetime I returned home to St. Louis from a 3-day business trip. I pulled into the garage and hauled my suitcase and briefcase into the house.

After I unpacked and got a TAB from the fridge, I went outside to collect my mail. Inside was a notice from the Post Office of an attempt to deliver a package. The next day during lunch, I drove to the PO to get my package.

When I opened the package – which was from Jim – I got the surprise of a lifetime. The contents of this package turned out to be my most precious possession. It is the one thing I would grab if my house was on fire and I could choose only one item to save. The contents of my package included a diary including pictures of our trip to Scotland.

The diary lists the courses we played, the meals we ate, the places we went, the odd things that happened during the trip. In short, it recounts our entire trip of a lifetime with my best friend in the entire world!

Men often have a difficult time expressing their feelings. When it comes to Jimmy, the depth of the feelings people have for him are like none I have ever seen. He has always been a friend who always puts the other person first.

Part of the attraction of this man is his brutal honesty. He calls them as he sees them.

July 4, 2008
(from Jimmy's website)

BODY, HEART AND SOUL
HAPPY FOURTH OF JULY

Body, heart and soul – three little words that one of the words, or two, or all three mean something to most people. All three mean a lot to me as I go through this horrible disease called ALS. My body is changing rapidly. I'm tired all the time. I am much weaker. I can't put my socks or shoes on by myself. I have to always be careful of not tripping because my left leg is so weak. I haven't eaten any solid food for 15 months. I have to take naps and use a machine to give me oxygen so I can talk throughout the day, as whenever I talk for awhile I have no breath left.

I can't walk upstairs unless I really push it and grab on to something. My talk is so slurry I'm embarrassed but we are getting a machine that will help me communicate. Honestly I'm tired of the regimen you saw that I go through everyday in Melanie's last update. She never says a word but I'm sure she is too and that depresses the hell out of me, more than what I have to go through. I've been through a lot, 3 knee operations, and in the last 4 years: prostate cancer, hepatitis C and the year long program to get rid of it. So I know my body pretty well and it's hard to admit that this little known, badly under funded and incurable disease is taking over my body. I've been a fighter my whole life but this time I'm up against unbeatable odds. This just doesn't seem right and that's just the body part.

The good news is that no matter what this disease does to me it will NEVER be able to take any part of my soul. I've lived a life basically helping people and that won't change. I have about 50 rose bushes and of course my wife and I like them but it gives me the opportunity to be able to brighten up some people's days. I live in a retirement area and the widows enjoy their "deliveries" so much it brings tears to your eyes. I've always tried to be polite to people as much as I can. I've always believed the more you give to other people, the more you will get in return. We live too much in I want it now, me – me – me society. It shouldn't be that way. We're supposed to help our fellow man.

This brings me to my last point. I've sent website updates out for a year now. I'm trying to educate people about ALS and raise money for the scientists, researchers and doctors who are desperately seeking funds to work on a cure for the disease. The problem is they can't get pharmaceutical money because it only affects about 30,000 people in the entire US and only about 5,000 people are diagnosed per year. What's worse is the time span from diagnosis to death is 1 to 5 years. I've already surpassed my "death date" from my original diagnosis. So there is no payoff for the big companies to invest millions and millions of dollars when there is no payback for them. Tough to look at it that way but as a businessman I completely understand it. That's why I am trying to raise as much money as I can to help the experts out, knowing that not one dime will help me. In quite a few of my updates I've tried to make people aware that every dollar counts no matter what they can give (and the minimum really is ONE dollar.) I've put it in as many different ways as I can think of.

I know it's tough times for a lot of people as the economy is not the best. For many people associated with this disease the accumulation of the donated dollars is the only way this horrible, terribly under funded, little known, incurable disease will ever have a chance to be cured. It will keep affecting people for no reason at all, be a tremendous strain on the diagnosed spouse, family and friends as well as being extremely expensive. Maybe it falls into the "it can't happen to me or my family or my friends" category that many people think.

It's one of two things that honestly makes me angry. There is another.

I look at all the people I've helped; some I've saved their businesses from going broke, some helping them make a very comfortable living and they've donated nothing. (Remember the minimum is ONE DOLLAR) I look at all the awards my program was given and how much good publicity it gave to the college. Even the highest administrative people at the college wrote and told me how much my program meant to the college and the community but they have basically donated a total amount so small from seven total people, it wouldn't pay most people's grocery bills for a month. And these people make VERY GOOD money.

My boss of 16 years, whose household's total annual income is at least $200,000 only gave $25.00. I could probably go down the list of my contacts and pick out a couple of hundred people that make more than $200,000 a year and know me but who have contributed nothing. But I keep sending them a note whenever there is a change in the website; hopefully they'll wake up someday and understand how good it feels to help people that need *help. It's the only other thing that does make me angry, our me-me-me selfish society.*

The lying is the other thing that gets me angry. I have been curious why some people have not given anything when I know they are well off. They say they give anonymously. I've had people tell me many people do give anonymously to my face, like they have. They're right. A lot of people do. The problem is I know the name of every person that has given anonymously. We just don't list their name as a donor. We list them as Anonymous, but I know who they are. To flat out lie to a dying person is pretty low in my book. Let's get on to happier things…

Jimmy has always called them as he sees them. It is one of the characteristics that made him an endeared teacher in the business community of Willamette Valley.

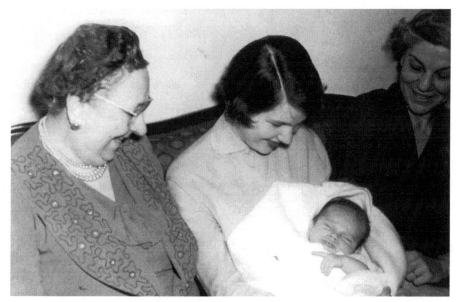

Nana, Mom and baby Jimmy

(Jimmy top left)
Andrew High School Sports Hall of Fame

Mac and Jimmy
Graduation Day at Corby's

(left to right)
JT and Jimmy cutting up in New Orleans

(left to right) Ty Taylor (died of ALS), Mike "Mac" McDonald (Jimmy's N.D. Roomate), Rich "Mez" Meznick, Shawn Culveyhouse (Jim's little sister), Jimmy, Anna Sturgill (Dee's daughter), Melanie, Dee Sturgill (Melanie's Sister), Jim "J.T." Terry

Jimmy's first home in Gary, Indiana

(left to right)
Two of Jimmy's Favorite People
Nick Thiros, Jimmy and Helen Thiros

Mean Joe Greene with Jimmy riding shotgun
at Diet Coke Launch in Detroit

Hanging out with The Champ
Jimmy, Evander Holyfield and Melanie

Jimmy in front of Hall of Fame

Jimmy and Chris Burskey at Royal St. Andrews
Jimmy shot 76

Jimmy and Melanie on a perfect football
weekend in front of "Touchdown Jesus"

Jimmy and Melanie at Bandon Dunes, Oregon

Jimmy in front of Positano's Ristorante
September 2007, 7 months after diagnosis

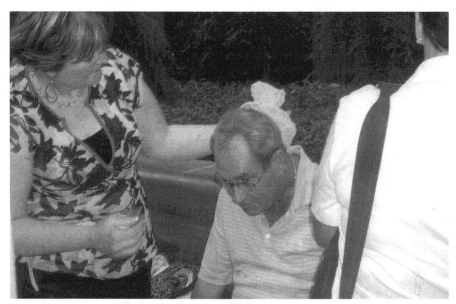

*Melanie comforting Jimmy after "Dumping" Jimmy
on 53rd Street in New York City*

Chris Stevens (author) and Jimmy

Teaching

Jimmy's business career included a lot of selling in the early years and a lot of teaching and coaching as he progressed up the corporate ladder. He always had a flare for the unexpected. During the Diet Coke introduction, Jimmy was given the challenge to handle all aspects of the launch to the Midwest bottling network. The venue was Detroit and, as always, Jimmy wowed them. Those in attendance felt it was the best Coke kick-off meeting ever. Jimmy had planned to build a huge display of Diet Coke, in the shape of a Diet Coke can. He neglected to remember that the organized labor environment of Michigan might make that difficult.

When the trucks arrived to deliver all the new Diet Coke cans, Jimmy was there to greet them as time was tight. As always, Jimmy had planned the logistics right down to the minute. Everyone had their checklist of "to dos." The only problem? No Coke employee was allowed to touch the product once the truck backed in.

After the truck backed in, all of the necessary arrangements had to be made to get the union responsible for unloading product in gear to get it done. But as the union members unloaded the goods, instead of moving toward the auditorium, they just left them on the dock. Sorry – to move the product into the facility was the jurisdiction of another local.

Jimmy greased the skids once again and finally the Diet Coke was headed to the auditorium. But once there, the thousands of cases of cans once again settled into a temporary resting place, as it was another local's responsibility to bring the product to the display area. And once there, with time slipping away, and Jimmy's thread of patience eroding, he learned that it was yet another local who was responsible for the actual construction of the display. Positioned behind a huge curtain, the display was erected in the nick of time.

The meeting went off without a hitch and everyone thought it was great. No one will ever forget when the curtains opened to the monstrous display and the entire marching band of the University of Michigan blew the lid off the place. Seems like a diminutive marketing manager from Coke paid a visit to the legendary head football coach "Bo' Schembechler himself and somehow persuaded him this was a great opportunity for the Big Blue.

Jimmy learned some valuable lessons with that event, such as not taking anything for granted. Over the years, Jimmy learned so many valuable lessons. He thought that one day he would love to teach and share his experiences with others.

When he decided to leave the corporate world, he first wanted to try his hand at running his own business. So Jimmy and Melanie opened a small gift shop retail business, Chuckles. He eventually expanded to three stores and Jimmy was named one of the top entrepreneurs of the year by the Oregon Small Business Association.

Jimmy also did his stint as a consultant, starting a Marketing company designed to train small businesses about the fundamentals of running a successful operation. Then, after all those years of pounding the pavement, working to hit the numbers, Jim found Chemeketa Community College – or should I say, it found him.

Chemeketa had a fledgling program that was designed to reach out to local businesses in central Oregon, but the response just wasn't there. He was asked to take it on for a try. The rest is history. I will let Jim explain in his own words.

I started out donating my time to counseling people who wanted to go into business. The head of the Small Business Management Program was retiring and it was a disaster. (Melanie went through it – they had about 8 businesses in the program.) The college president, who was a friend of mine, approached me and asked if I would redo the program to make it more saleable and to better help the business community and thus their relationship with the college. I agreed and said I'd do it for a year.

When I got into it, I knew a major alteration was needed and I changed it completely after surveying the business community. I changed it to one two-hour visit from me once a month and one night per month I secured a qualified expert speaker in their field to speak on a particular topic that was needed by the business owners. I knew a lot of people so I basically sold the speakers on community service and how they might even get some clients out of it. (They did.) Marketing, Insurance, Estate planning, Sales, Savings and Retirement planning, Communication, Human Relations and Employees, How to handle the media, just about everything... you name it.

The first one on one meeting I would get to know their business and in the second we developed a "game plan." Then, for the next 7 months we tried to accomplish their goals. The first night I was always the speaker. I outlined how the program worked and then did a seminar on time management, short and long term planning, short and long term goals (written down), how to be a list person and how important it was to organize your life and have all your important documents and wishes in one folder as usually only one of the spouses does all the bookkeeping and the other doesn't have a clue.

Sixteen years ago I think we charged $100 for the program. When I left, we charged $595 and it was still the best bargain around. Every year we picked 30 businesses to be in the program and I never had one complaint except people said we should charge even more. The program lasted for 9 months and we had a celebration dinner at the end of the program for the businesses' husbands and wives. The program was a hit and even though I committed to one year I really enjoyed helping people and did it for 16 years. It was nice to be recognized with many awards for the program and it was written up in the paper almost every year.

I was fortunate to help many businesses. I particularly want to acknowledge Gail Gable who has really turned around his printing business, still saving time to coach high school basketball at the most competitive level.

John Mills runs a concrete company. A terrific guy with a heart of gold, John has always been willing to listen and learn. He is the perfect example of what an entrepreneur should be. Someone once said: "If you think you are too big to do the little job, then you are probably too little to do the big job." John has always been willing to take counsel and always is willing to lead by example.

My good friend Steve Rentfro runs a bark and dusting business. Steve has been able to find a niche and make a good living by focusing on service and quality. He is willing to walk away from jobs he knows do not play to his core competency. But when he takes on a job, he puts a full court press on getting it done right.

Kathy and Jack Dalton have done a great job of transforming their playground equipment company into the vendor of choice for many municipalities. They were willing to really change how they were doing business and dare into the unchartered waters of changing their model… and it worked.

Dave Boyles owns the Sassy Onion Restaurant in Salem. His attention to detail is unbelievable and he has a full court press on quality food served at a value price. He does very well in the function business and if you want to find him, don't bother looking for him on a golf course. The odds are you will find him with an apron on either cooking or testing food in the kitchen or working the tables to ensure his patrons are happy.

Robert Kraft has a remodeling business. I can't thank Robert enough for his generosity in donating to ALS research. He is one of the single largest donors to the ALS fund raising campaign in my name.

I am not sure what to say about Lisa Vegas. Lisa has her own catering business. We met through the program and have become the best of friends. I respect Lisa as much as any business person I have ever known and I care for Lisa as much as I care for my best friends. What started as a teacher-student relationship has evolved into a two member mutual admiration society.

I have many stories of small businesses I feel I have helped. One of my favorite stories is about a lady in a very small community in Gates, OR. She had a small pottery business that made little knick-knacks and sold them all over the world. Her business was growing so fast, she needed a loan which I helped her get.

But to manage the growth she needed people as well and I did everything I could to put her in touch with some good candidates who could help her. The problem was the business was growing so fast, cash flow was always a problem. So her husband, an ex-logger went back to logging with the plan of doing it for six months. They would have health insurance for themselves and their employees with the savings. After six months he'd quit and they would be able to afford it themselves as a company. She was one of the few that took my "organizing your life" seriously the first night and did it.

Unfortunately after two months her husband was crushed by a loader and died instantly. But she had her folder and went to a lawyer. I spent a lot of extra time with her and after explaining to the college her situation, we were able to help her out. Bottom line everything was taken care of and the lawyer even asked if he could copy my forms to hand out to all his clients. A tragic situation that turned out OK and I always mentioned the story the first night of the program as everybody always thinks "it won't happen to me."

In my course I developed a list of 10 Rules for Success. I want to share them with you. I lifted this right out of my course program. I have shared this list with all of my business students. I hope you find it helpful.

Top 10 Rules for Success

> *1. Always be nice to people. The old saying; Do unto others… is not enough. Go beyond that; the more you give, the more you will get in return.*

When I graduated from Notre Dame my first job was with the Gallo Wine Company. I was the first college graduate that they hired right out of college. I knew I had to make a name for myself because I didn't know anything about wine, but I did know how people like to be treated. Back in the mid-70's wine was only displayed in the liquor departments in grocery stores which is what division I was in. I had 30 stores that I was to "service" every week. Service meant clean the bottles and keep the shelves clean and maybe get the liquor manager to give you a display which we were graded on by the company; a disadvantage was how young I was. I had to come up with a plan. I bought a little cardholder that your mom keeps her favorite recipe index cards in. I made up a card for each store. Every time I went in to the store I made it a point to talk to somebody new in the store each time; starting with the manager of the store. I kept track of things they liked, things about their family, what their interests were outside of the grocery business, etc. Anything I could pick up from them and write it down in the car when I got there. Then the next time I was in the store I would go say hi to them and ask them how their yard was doing, how their kids (by name) were doing, etc. In time I'd ask the dairy department head if we could put up a little display of wine because cheese and wine were such a natural combination, same with the meat department guy and on and on. All of a sudden I had displays all over the store and was setting huge records for displays with the company. Mr. Gallo himself even came down to ride with me one day to see what my "secret" was. Obviously he was amazed, and said "son you're going places". People only buy things for two reasons; one because they need, want or could use the product you're selling or two, because they like the person selling it to them. That's it, the mystery of sales unfounded. You be the nicest and know how to communicate with them on things they are interested in and know their name and you'll win every time.

2. Never lie. If you don't know the answer, admit it, and tell the person you'll research their question and get back to them. Make sure you do, in a timely fashion. (no more than 24 hours) Those who lie have to keep lying to cover up another lie and all of a sudden they don't know what the truth really is or was.

3. When you say you are going to do something, do it and give the person a reasonable time frame when it will be done. Always under promise and over deliver, this also means always be on time for appointment. If your appointment is at 9AM and you arrive at 9AM you are 5 minutes late. Being late only tells the person you are meeting that your time is more important than theirs. That's a bad, bad start to an appointment.

4. Return phone calls, e-mails and texts in a timely fashion. My rule was always to promise I will return your inquiry within 24 hours. If the person took their time to contact you, it's your duty to give them the respect of answering in a timely fashion.

5. Always have written short term and long term goals. They have to be written down with a date that they need to be completed by and what is your plan of action to get the task done. Always take big projects and break them down to as little as you know you can commit to with no excuse not to attain and finish them. Once you gather all your little completions you will have an easy time putting them all together and accomplishing your goal. The key is commitment and keeping to your plan, never say I'll make it up tomorrow, make it a priority for today, no matter what. Become a reasonable list maker. 10 minutes of planning the night before will save you lots of unproductive time the next day. It's absolutely amazing how much people waste time. They think they are working but because they have no plan for the day, the day runs them. One of my favorite clients who resisted lists for years finally started doing them. After 6 months I received the ultimate compliment from her: "I now get twice as much done in a day in half the time". In business it's called letting the business run you instead of you running your business.

6. Always plan for the unexpected. Never think it can't happen to you or your family. It can. Only one person knows and He is not going to give you a warning. Life is a four legged stool when it comes to finances. Current fixed bills, the ones that you can't do anything about are easy to plan for; mortgages, utility bills, groceries, etc. They come every month and you know about how much they will be. Plan for them. You can do this on a piece of paper or by a spreadsheet program on a computer.

Second are discretionary bills; those are the ones you have a choice about. Now unfortunately I think

*our society has become an "I want it now no mat-
ter what" society. Maybe that's why bankruptcies
are at an all time high. Since credit card debt is
also at an all time high I think it will just get worse
because people with high interest credit card debt
quite frankly will never get out of debt because of
the interest they are paying. This should be taught
at every high school in America but even more
in every law, doctors, dentist's schools, etc. – all
professional schools as they are some of the worst
at finances that I encountered. They are great at
their craft but terrible as businessmen. I always
saved up for something that I wanted so I can pay
in cash, no interest for those credit card companies which are really banks. They make enough
money. Why should I help them make more? And
I've never found anything that I couldn't wait for
or a "deal of a lifetime" that I couldn't wait to
get until I had the money. And I won't even get
into going out to eat four or five times a week, or
every lunch. How many coffees you consume? Get
the idea?*

*Now we've only looked at two legs of our stool.
What about the other two? Are you ever going to
retire? The amount of money people have at an
age close to retirement age in our country is ap-
palling. 36% of working adults have not started
to save for retirement. An additional 16% have
saved less than $10,000, and 17% have saved
between 16,000 and $49,999. Believe me forget
the debates on whether social security will be
here or not. You will not be able to live solely off
your social security and you pay taxes on what
you receive. As of 2004 the average annual Social
Security retirement benefit was about $11,000.*

Only 20% of Americans have a pension down from 40% in 1975. Pretty grim statistics, I'd say. How are people going to live? Everybody needs to set up a retirement plan as early as they possibly can. I set one up for my niece and nephew at birth and contribute on the birthdays and Christmas. There is a wonderful part of finances called "compounding interest". Luckily my father taught it to me at a very young age. If you don't understand, ask a financial consultant, your banker, a math teacher – they will all explain it to you until you understand it for free. Free is a very good price for something that will control the rest of your life.

The last leg is different for each person because people are different. What makes up this leg? Do you have children? Have you seen college expenses now? What will they be when your newborn is ready as a senior in high school?

What about a "rainy day" fund if something goes wrong? Have you ever had a washer, dryer, air conditioner, etc. go out at exactly the wrong time? Having to buy something immediately out of necessity is painful- no searching for the best deal, I've got to have it now. Not the best way to get a good deal or the smartest.

Shouldn't you be able to have some fun in your life and reward yourself and family with a nice vacation? Of course you can but again you have to save for it. No enjoy it now and pay for it later.

The last question of this leg is the most personal. I've seen hundreds and hundreds of tax returns of people that make very good money and what they give to their church and/or charity is down-right pitiful. Everybody has their idea of what they should give to their church and/or charity. My wife and I at marriage made a vow that we would give a percentage of what we made to our church and to charity and have stuck by it for 25+ years. Most Mormons give 10% which is admi-rable. Ours is a little higher but we never had children so we could do a little more. The amount is not the question, the thought and commitment are what is important. We owe it to our fellow man that has a bad break, a medical condition that needs helping. There are hundreds and hun-dreds of charities and medical facilities that do great work but need money desperately. It's your duty as a human to contribute to others as well as your church; the more you give the more you will get in return.

7. Stay out of debt as much as you possibly can. Credit cards if not paid off every month are the biggest waste of money there is. Again, if you don't have the money, don't buy it. Save up and then buy it. Everything can wait. There are thousands of well known successful companies that have gone out of business and worse, they were making good money. There is an easy tracking and plan-ning device that I think is the most important tool for an individual or business. It's called a Cash Flow Sheet. It's run on the very basic philosophy of tracking when and how much money comes in and when, how much, and to where it went. I have put together a simple cash flow sheet for your help. They are at the end of this section. I de-scribe how it works on those pages. The first page is for people without or access to a computer, the second is for the people that do. If you can do it on a computer it is such a advantage as you have the formulas for an Excel spreadsheet already put in for you and you can add as many income and expenses as you want The other and neatest feature is you can play around with it without erasing, the computer does it for you. If you still have problems call a SBDC (Small Business Development Center for help – free) the one I was involved with was here in Salem, OR and the number is 503-399-5088 or 503-399-5181. Tell them you need to find a SBDC Center near your home. Feel free to mention my name. They will help you and if you're nice maybe even help you by phone.

8. Do you have a will or trust? Do you have a succession plan for your business that you or even your ancestors put so much time and effort to build up? If not, why not? Not enough time? Don't need to right now? I'm in good health, I'll do it later. Same excuses over and over, no commitment and nothing will happen to me. I call it something else, stupidity. What would happen to your family and/ or business if you died tonight? Most couples and owners have one person that that keeps the books, pays the bills, etc. The problem I've seen hundreds of times and almost every time the other spouse or owner doesn't have a clue how "that stuff" works or worse has no idea how to read them or what they mean. Who is ultimately responsible? No not your accountant. YOU are, so I'd start learning what goes into those "numbers".

9. Which brings me to the most important book a family/and or business needs to keep in one 3 ringer binder, as it could be and probably will be thee most important book you own. It's called an organizer of your life. It needs to have every important paper in it that you own and it needs to be in one place because who knows what is going to transpire that somebody will desperately need it. What if your spouse dies unexpectedly and you start getting asked a bunch of questions that you can't answer? What's worse- when is the absolutely worst time to try to talk or try to remember these things? That's right- when you are in state of shock and grief. What if both parents go down in a place crash? What about the children that somebody took care of while you were gone? You have to keep a book with details.

10. Where do the relatives or executor start with the unbelievable job of sorting through what the parents owned or owed? Birth certificates, Social security numbers, insurance policies, car titles, stocks, mutual funds, bank certificates, wills, trusts, powers of attorney, medical directives, appendices- to whom do you want precious heirlooms given? What bills come in and when, when are they due and where are they to mailed to; what are the account numbers of everything you pay or own; who can someone call that would be of help; an accountant, lawyer, banker, insurance agent, financial consultant? I could go on and on but this is, in my opinion, the most important possession you will have. I had a client whose business was growing and growing so fast they needed to start offering some type of health insurance for their employees and themselves, or they were not going to be able to employ the type of people they needed. The family made a decision that the husband who used to be a logger would go back to logging for six months and they would have enough money for him to come back to the business. They would have enough for a health plan for themselves and their employees. Tragically one day the husband slipped and was crushed to the death by a logging truck. Luckily the wife had taken my advice and had put together an organizer book. While she was in total grief she handed it over to her lawyer who put all the wheels in motion. He even called me and asked if he could copy my organizer so he could give out to every client he had to recommend that they fill it out too. That made me feel good- for the wife and kids of the deceased husband and the lawyer's clients- if they listened and committed to the project, they would benefit also.

11. Always keep the best for last. I'm going to just give you a list of things you should think about. Every person is different but in many ways we should be the same. We all know what's right or wrong. But there are so many other things that most people should incorporate into their daily lives instead of just letting their day run them. Here's a few:

- *If you see somebody that needs help, help them. Just the other day I saw an elderly, crippled woman trying to cross the street downtown. It was obvious she wasn't going to make it before the light turned red. A young man with spiked blue hair and a lot of jewelry in various places ran out and escorted her to the other side of the street- it made me feel like there's hope out there.*

- *Try to smile all the time, even on the phone. Smile while you are opening a door for someone and if someone does something nice to you always say thank you. I have written a personal thank you to every single person that has contributed to my ALS research drive. Why? – It's the right thing to do. Teach your children the words no ma'am, yes ma'am, no sir, yes sir, please and thank you and they will be ahead of 95% of the other children they are competing against in life.*

- *Always think of others. I have spent an incredible amount of time in doctors' offices and hospitals in the last five years. I've never felt sorry for myself because I always see people that are worse off than me. I always have a kind word for all the people that work in these environments. Do you know how tough their work is? They don't exactly get people that are thrilled to be there so they might be a little on edge, so I always take the time to say hello or say thanks for the job they do.*

- *Children are precious little people; spend time with them. It means so much more than money. They seek attention and care and if you decided to become a parent it's your job to give them what they need emotionally.*

- *What you give emotionally, spiritually, and financially to others you will get back twice in return.*

- *Always be optimistic. Every day I wake up it is a good day, no matter how I feel*

Jimmy has taught more than six hundred businesses in Oregon how to be better, how to be more organized, how to invest smarter, how to hire better people. Professor Schwartz at Brandeis taught so many students about life before being diagnosed with ALS. Jimmy has done the same with scores of businesses whose future depended on sound advice. To talk to some of those people Jimmy mentioned above was a privilege. Jimmy Culveyhouse made a difference not only in their businesses but in their lives.

Jimmy's one constant companion these past twenty-six years has been Melanie. Her support helped Jimmy become successful with the Chuckles store. She helped Jimmy with the course he taught for sixteen years. She is a brilliant woman with an amazing work ethic and a heart of gold. Jimmy paid tribute to her as his health was failing.

August 18, 2008
(from Jimmy's website)

My wife has been a complete angel. This is what I wrote on my web site for her birthday:

As my disease progresses, which it is, I'm losing more and more stamina and it's getting harder to breathe, I'd like to tell you about the most remarkable woman I've ever met. Why today – it's her birthday. When I asked what she wanted she said, "For more people to consider a $1 (the least) or more to your ALS Fundraising, as they have no idea what this horrible, under funded and little known incurable disease does to the diagnosed, their families and their friends."

As special days occur, I can tell you when you are in the downward slide of your life, special occasions become much more meaningful. It's like crossing another barrier that you made and once you make that one, now what's the next one?

I call this lady Mother Theresa. I could fill pages of why but I'll just outline a few things:

She helped raise her sisters at a very young age

She has always been around to help someone in need

She was there for all 4 of one of her sister's children's births

She went back and forth to San Antonio for 4 years when another sister, Tina, had cancer and unfortunately passed away. One year she made 17 round trips to help take care of the children in San Antonio

She was there for my sister's, Shawn, first birth, Prescott, and flew home after the birth. Unfortunately my sister developed some complications over night and Melanie got on a plane the next day and went back for another week.

She took care of Prescott during my sister's second birth, Aubree, my godchild, so Alex, my brother in law and Shawn could spend more time together and didn't have to worry about the day to day care of a three-year-old.

She and I have now taken two of our nieces into our home permanently to give them a better chance with their education and to open more of their possibilities than they could in Guadalajara.

During all these years she kept working

She went through 25+ years of my shenanigans

And now she's faced with the hardest, most time consuming horrible experience of all, to take care of her dying husband, which if you haven't read one of the past updates go back and see what a normal day is for the two of us together. And it's only going to get worse. Does she show any of her frustrations? Nope. Her only problem is her problem she has had forever; she can't say NO. Weddings, bridal parties, baby showers, you name it; she's always ready to help and everyone wants her because she's so talented.

Well I found a little poem to honor her on her day:

My Loving Wife

*You've been there
to laugh with me
to cry with me,
to be proud of me,
and to be happy for all
the good things in my life...*

*You've shared my disappointments
and listened and helped me
through difficult times.
You're
the most important part of my life...
and you always will be.
I Love you.*

*I give thanks to God always
for you...
I Corinthians 1:4*

There's an old expression, I'd rather be lucky than good, and I hit a grand slam on having Melanie as my wife. She truly is one in a million.

In all honesty I'm not ready to die quite yet. I've worked really hard on getting our affairs in order. We've taken a total pro-active approach. Our house has been remodeled to ADA standards with the help of some very good friends. We've made the upstairs very accommodating for our nieces that live with us. We have a great circle of friends that are willing to help at any time. I want to raise more money for ALS research; I want to have all the fundraising in a way that anybody could do it without me and continue to do so.

I want to make sure everything is in perfect order for Melanie. I want to be more comfortable at Melanie being able to handle the finances. And finally I want to plan the greatest "Irish Wake" (not funeral, not a Celebration of Life which would be the closest thing to what I have planned.) An Irish Wake is a party, a celebration, and I have plans for one helluva' send off. I want people to remember me for my zest for life, my kindness to my fellow man, and to make people happy even when the circumstance doesn't call for it. One of my clients sent me the following which is the most cherished thing I ever received (except Melanie). It reads:

You're one of my true heroes in life. Let me describe what I mean by hero.

Someone I look up to.

Someone that tries to be nice to everyone.

Someone that has helped me personally.

Someone that has helped me spiritually.

Someone that has given to me without wanting in return.

Someone that has helped my business and my family.

Someone I long to know more of.

Someone I will see in heaven and enjoying the Big party.

Dave Boyles; owner of The Sassy Onion Restaurant; Salem, OR

THE ONLY BIG PROBLEM I HAVE IS THAT THE WORST IS YET TO COME AND IT AIN'T GOOD AND THERE'S NOT A DAMN THING ANYBODY CAN DO ABOUT IT. THE WORST IS THAT IT AFFECTS OTHER PEOPLE AROUND ME, AND MOSTLY THE LOVE OF MY LIFE, AND THAT MAKES ME EXTREMELY SAD! IT'S PLAIN AND SIMPLE: ALS SUCKS!

Steve Viale and Creekside Country Club

When Jim speaks of his best friends, he mentions several: Mez, former "co-pilot" and mentor at Gallo; J.T, his running mate at Coke; and Chris Burskey, his favorite Coca-Cola sidekick. As Jimmy moved to new locations in his life, more friends would follow. Jimmy just has a way of impacting those around him so much, they just want to be in his presence – people like Peter and Robin Juhren and a quiet, slender, single-digit handicap golfer at Creekside Country Club named Steve Viale.

When Jimmy and Melanie moved to Salem, Oregon, they found a place they could really call home. Jimmy's passion for golf was one shared by Melanie as well. With no children to raise, free time has been spent in the company of friends in the Salem area. After playing several courses in the area, a new one was opening up not far from their home. Presented with this idyllic opportunity, Jimmy became one of the founding members of Creekside Country Club in Salem. He credits his good friend, pro golfer Peter Jacobson, for tipping him off to the Creekside opportunity.

Private golf country clubs are not for everyone. Those who seek them enjoy the camaraderie of regular tee times with friends and social evenings with the spouses. Situated on a hill in the southeastern section of Salem, Creekside is simply a slice of heaven and it was here where Jimmy would build another lifelong friendship.

Steve Viale is a slender man. I don't want to say he is thin, but if you put a red tie around his neck, he'd look like a thermometer. With a little make-up he could enter and probably place in a looka-like contest for the late George Carlin. And he is just a great guy with a great sense of humor and affection for his friend.

On my first trip to Salem, Jimmy set up a meeting with Steve. He arrived punctually. We struggled a bit through some awkward moments as I turned on the dicta-phone and asked him if he minded if I recorded our conversation. Answering like a true friend of Stump's, he deadpanned, "No problem."

Steve is Jimmy's main golf partner at Creekside. The entrance to the club sits exactly 195 yards away from the front door of Jimmy and Melanie's home. There is a wire fence with some vines on it protecting the fifteenth green from passers by. Only a couple of years ago, Jimmy, if he wished, could drop a Pro V-1 on his lawn and smooth a five iron to that green. Creekside is Jimmy's second home and Jimmy is close to Creekside and so many members there.

But no one at Creekside feels more for Jimmy than slender Steve.

Stump and Steve have won their fair share of hardware and gentle-manly wagers at Creekside, but the most memorable was the last one they entered.

Jimmy was diagnosed with ALS in February 2007. By the time April rolled around, Jimmy's symptoms were obvious to all he knew. At Creekside, though, you would never know it. It was business – or rather, pleasure as usual. Golf has provided Jimmy with welcome relief to the grueling Bataan death march he is on. And Steve Viale has been with him every step of the way.

When it came time for the sign-up for the Spring Senior 2-Ball Club Championship, Jimmy and Steve decided, "What the heck," and entered. While Jimmy's speech was slurred and he was by then featuring a noticeable stagger to his gait, he could still swing a golf club. Distance started to suffer. He was no longer 285 off the tee, but his short game was as good as ever.

As improbable as Kirk Gibson hitting a walk-off home run in the 1985 World Series on basically one leg, or Tiger Woods winning the U.S. Open in 2008 on an even worse leg, Steve and Stump rung up one more championship at Creekside "for the Gipper." They did not just win the "low gross" score, they won the "low net" as well, an amazing feat for two low single digit handicappers.

There wasn't a dry in the place when they accepted the award.

After the dinner, Steve headed to the parking lot. After storing some of his gear in his trunk, he slammed it shut and glanced to his left. Jimmy was standing alone in the lot near his car just standing there. In his arms were both of the awards he and Steve had just won. Viale meandered over to his motionless partner whose head was bowed looking down at the hardware.

When Steve came alongside Jimmy, Stump looked up and there were tears streaming down his cheeks. He looked into Steve's eyes which were now also filled with tears and quietly spoke. "This award means more to me than any other I have ever won. Thank you, Steve. I love you, Bro."

With those words, the two embraced a long hard hug. Two grown men weeping in each others arms in the Creekside parking lot – it is a moment that almost two years later still brings tears to Steve's eyes.

As Steve relates more stories he becomes increasingly more emotional. It is obvious the bond they share is as strong as Crazy Glue. One story that makes Steve still laugh to this day is when he hit his shot literally into a tree and Jimmy refused to give him a free drop. Steve had to play it from the tree, much to the delight of his mischievous companion.

But Steve's favorite occurred in the spring of 2008.. It was pretty clear that the number of future rounds of golf in Stump's remaining life would be very few. But the inseparable two-some were playing a round one day and Jimmy was struggling with his short game. Chip shots were coming up short and he missed several putts that in olden days he probably would have drained. After missing yet another makeable try with the flat stick, Steve started to walk to the golf cart, certain not to say anything to make things even worse for his partner.

As he arrived at the cart and began to holster his weapons, he looked next to him ready to now console Jimmy after the awkward silence. But… no Jimmy. He looked around and then turned back to the green he had just left. There stood Jimmy in the same spot where he had left him. He was immobile, gazing skyward.

Steve hustled back over to see if Jimmy was alright. As he walked, he never took his eyes off Jimmy and Jimmy never took his eyes off of the sky. Just as he was about to say something, Jimmy began reaching his arms skyward as if beseeching the Lord and he bellowed, "Is it too much to ask to give me one stinking putt? Why hast thou forsaken me?" Then he shook his head and trudged back to the cart.

Memories of Peter Finch in the award-winning movie *Network*: "I want you to go to your window and I want you to shout out, 'I'm mad as hell and I'm not going to take it anymore.'"

ALS has taken from Jimmy one of his greatest gifts – his amazing golf game. He has every right to be mad as hell.

When I asked Steve if there was something he wanted to say, a story to tell or something he wanted me to write about the two of them, Steve responded, "Let me think about it. I will send you something." Three weeks later in the mail I received a letter from Steve, remembering his friend Jimmy and a special day.

My Day With Jim

It started out innocently enough with a phone call to see if we were going golfing. I could tell from his hello the answer was going to be no. I had been nursing some cracked ribs so I wasn't terribly disappointed, but I told him I would stop by later to chat.

I keep my word and during our chat he asked if I would do a beer run for him, as I had done many times before... only the beer run means returning all the empty cans also. Well this time apparently the Culveyhouse household had been VERY thirsty because by the time I loaded them in the car I could barely see out the windows.

Off to Safeway I go praying a cop doesn't pull me over cause I'd never be able to talk my way out of the open container law. I make it to Safeway and go in to get a cart and grab the first one I see. What I didn't notice until I got back to the car is that it was a kiddy cart with the seats at the front for 2 kids. Well I wasn't going back to exchange it so I loaded it up and this cart is now overflowing with cans and bottles, even filled the kiddy seats up.

I hoped I wouldn't see anyone I knew as I was getting some strange looks from the SUV moms. I must have looked like a homeless guy cashing in his week's work. Just as I am about at the front door I hear "Viale is that you?" Great... just what I need.

Over comes my friend Dianne and she wants to talk. So there I am in the entrance to Safeway with a kiddy cart full of beer cans and bottles and all these people going in and out trying to avoid the homeless guy. Terrific. And I can tell Dianne isn't buying my explanation of bringing all these back for a friend. By now I don't give a darn.

I get into the return room with all the machines and I put the first Perrier bottle in. Unfortunately I put it in backwards and it jammed up the machine and I could hear it crushing the glass and the next thing I know it starts firing out the shards of glass back out the chute. I run for cover as that damn thing just keeps shooting glass all over the room. I felt like I was in Baghdad. Thank God no one else was in the room as I could have killed them.

The machine finally runs out of ammo and I quickly stuff all the rest in and get my tickets, go get the 12 beers, pay and head for the car. Can't find my keys and I then realize I had them in my hand when I put that first bottle in and in the heat of battle had dropped them in the chute.

So I head back to the store, get the manager to get the janitor to come open the machine. He walks into the room looks around at the war scene and says, "Damn kids just come in and break up bottles just for fun. I'd love to catch them at it just once." I meekly agree with him, thank him for my keys and get the hell out of there before they examine the security video.

Amazingly the beer is still on the hood when I get back to the car. I have to put it in the passenger side rear door as the driver's side rear door doesn't work anymore. So I put his beer in his paper bag and his fricking precious 8 year old boxes.

I take the kiddy-cart back which now reeks of stale beer. I get in to start the car and take off only to hear this horrendous sound of metal on concrete. I look back and see that in my haste I forgot to close the rear door. Oh well, the light post took care of that for me. I am dumbfounded at my own stupidity. I finally get to Jimmy's house to unload the beer. The front door is locked and he has left the garage door open just enough for a circus midget to get under it and I with my cracked ribs try to squeeze in screaming out in agonizing pain. Finally I pop thru and go to open the door to bring everything in. I hit the door opener/closer figuring I can run under it and let it close. Not!!!

I have to jump over infrared sensor crack my head on the damn door knocking me to the ground landing on my cracked ribs. I lay there a while trying to gain senses. I get to my knees and there right in front of me is the car door with a 2 foot high crease running the entire length of the door. Then the door opens and Jimmy sees me and says, "What the hell took you so long?"

I just start laughing, thinking this is my reward for helping my bud and I decide right there I will never fix that door. It will always be a reminder of "my day with Jim."

Steve Viale is a man of few words. He loves Jimmy like a brother. He, like so many others, hates to watch this special man have to endure the pain and suffering. Steve is very close to Jimmy, but no two friends are closer to Melanie and Jimmy now than the Juhrens.

Peter and Robin

Peter and Robin Juhren live in the Salem area and they, as a couple, are as close to Jim and Melanie as you can get. They love having meals together, drinking wine, and seeing who can put the others down the most. It is pure love.

One of Stump's wish list items on his "bucket list" was to see New York City one more time. By the time September 2007 had rolled around, the effects of Jim's ALS were not just noticeable, they were dramatically affecting his ability to function. Eating was no longer an option as he had a hole put in his chest so that nutrients could enrich his body as he slept each night. The capacity of his lungs was starting to dissipate – a sure sign of the advancing intentions of the disease. But one more big weekend was in order.

While Jimmy loves golf, his affection for tennis is also noteworthy. He was inducted into the Andrean High School Sports Hall of Fame for tennis as well as golf. Peter and Robin along with two other close friends, Ellen and Lee Vaterlaus, organized a weekend in Manhattan and Queens to see the US Open.

Peter tells it best in his own words:

> *Jim had always discussed with me his deep desire to one day go to the US Open tennis tournament held every year in Flushing Meadows, NY, around the end of August through Labor day.*

After his diagnosis with ALS in February 2007, we decided that this would be the year. Melanie, Jim, Ellen and Lee Vaterlaus, and my wife Robin and I started to plan the trip that little did we know would be the "trip of a lifetime" for us all.

Chapter 1   "You did what?"

Once all the plans were finalized, we ended up taking the red eye from Portland, OR, connecting through Atlanta and arriving in NY the next morning. Celebratory cocktails at the bar before we left, everyone was excited to get going. We finally walked down to the departure gate where Jim declared that he had to use the rest room. After about 10 minutes we started to get concerned and just as we were about to go look for him, he appeared.

"Where were you?" Melanie and I asked. "In the bathroom" was the reply. No big deal, but then Jim stated, "I was smoking." We were all floored. "What do you mean you were smoking? Have you lost your mind?" we all exclaimed. "What if you got caught?" Jim's simple and methodical reply was, "If you stand next to the toilet and keep flushing no one can smell it as the smoke goes down with the water."

Chapter 2   "We'll catch the next one"

We departed Portland late and as we had a tight connection in Atlanta we figured we would miss that flight and get booked on the next one. After arriving in Atlanta, everyone made a pit stop at the restrooms and we grabbed a coffee on the go. We took our time and headed on down to the departure gate. No one was in a hurry so we kind of meandered our way there. As we approached the gate, they were actually in the process of final boarding, and there were about six people lined up waiting to board (they obviously were on standby). We were shocked that the plane was actually even still here, so as we approached the ticket agent asked if we had booked seats on this flight and we said we did. You could hear the moans and groans of the passengers who were sure they were about to clear standby only to be deflated when we showed at the last minute. And all Jimmy could say was, "I bet they're pissed at us, but too bad."

Chapter 3　　*"Would you like a mini-tour of New York City?"*

We arrived in NY around 8:30AM and we had arranged for a private car to pick us up. As we came down the escalator there was the driver with his name sign and we introduced ourselves. Jimmy declared that he "wanted a smoke" and the driver was in full agreement, so while they went to collect the vehicle and partake in a cigar, the rest of us rounded up the luggage. After all was loaded, we piled into the van for what we expected to be a 15 minute ride into Midtown Manhattan. In the 15 minutes it took to get the luggage, Jimmy had become best friends with the driver, Vladimir, which actually surprised no one.

Vladimir asked if we were in a hurry to get to the hotel and if not he would be happy to give us a short tour of the city. Robin and I, having grown up in New York, were against this idea as there are as many scams in New York as there are buildings, but Jimmy was insistent and so off we went for the tour.

Our first stop was Harlem, which has changed dramatically in the past 25 years. We drove past the infamous Apollo Theater and then on to Columbia University. Onward through upper Manhattan we toured, all the time our Russian tour guide is telling us about all the brownstones he owns throughout the city. I will say he was very charismatic and he was knowledgeable. And he and Jimmy were already best friends or long lost brothers or something along those lines...a multi-million dollar property owner, doubtful.

We eventually arrived at our destination, the Hilton Midtown on 6th Ave. at 53rd St. A two hour tour, Jimmy with a new friend, and most of us ready for a shower and something to eat. Hopefully our rooms are ready...

Chapter 4   *"Whadaya mean you ain't on da same floor?"*

We booked our trip as a package through Steven Furgal's Tennis Tours and the Hilton was one of the hotels offered. We approached the check-in desk and inquired about our rooms. As I am a Hilton Diamond member, my room was ready but the others would not be available until later in the afternoon, so we decided I would check in, we could dump all of the luggage in our room, and at least go out and get a bite to eat. As we were rounding up our stuff, Ventura, one of the bellmen, approached us and asked if we needed assistance. We explained we were going to put all the baggage in our room and if he could assist that would be great. I stated that our room was ready, the others were not, but we knew where everyone would be as far as rooms go. He looked at the room assignments and said "Wait a minute! You guys ain't even close to each other. Come with me, we'll take care of this right now."

Back to the check-in desk and Ventura worked feverishly and with great expertise in tandem with the desk girl to relocate us so we all could be close. After 10 minutes of shuffling and directing, he proudly announced we had three rooms all on the same floor, two right next to each other and one just one door down. As in all of NY, it ain't what you know but who you know. After delivering all our bags, Ventura made it clear if we needed anything all we needed to do was get a hold of him anytime... for anything. So we all checked into our rooms happily. Robin and I were in room 2251.

Chapter 5   *"The Pothole"*

We decided to do a bit of sightseeing as we were all fresh and fed, so we decided to head over towards Rockefeller Center. We were on the corner of 6th and 53rd waiting to cross. As Jimmy was tired, we had him sitting in "Hugo" (a wheeled walker with a seat) and Melanie was pushing him. As the signal changed and we were able to go, I looked down to see a small pothole about the size of a donut in the street and the wheel of Hugo just behind it. Before I could get the words out to "Stop!" Melanie started to push and into the hole the wheel of Hugo went. This in turn caused the unit to flip over, and at the same time dump Jimmy over backwards onto 53rd St. His head bounced off the road and he winced in pain. But before any of us could bend over to help him, 10 people were there helping him up, checking him over, and offering any assistance they could.

His head was bleeding pretty badly, and Melanie suggested we call 911. I asked Jim if he was dizzy at all, and he said he wasn't. Just then a doctor walked up and started to ask Jim questions. He looked at his head and stated that it was bleeding quite a bit but was not as serious as we thought. Melanie still thought we should call 911 but Jim was against it. We knew he was OK when he looked at Mel and said, "I can't believe you dumped me out onto 53rd St.!"

I took off to a Duane-Reade drugstore to get some gauze, bandages, and antibacterial cream. When I returned, a street vendor working the corner had given Mel water and napkins to help clean Jim up. We dressed his wounds, got him up, and headed back to the hotel to get Jim changed. I approached the street vendor and offered to pay for the water but he refused to take any. I pleaded but he refused.

Even though this was all at Jim's expense, Jim, Melanie, Ellen and Lee saw the side of New Yorkers most people never get to see. When someone is in need they will rally without hesitation.

Chapter 6   "It's still in the bush"

After dinner Jim, Lee and I would step outside and have a cigar. This was kind of a tradition even back home when we would get together. I never really enjoy smoking any more than half a cigar, so when I was done I sat it down in the ashtray. Jim looked at me like I threw $10.00 in the garbage pail. "How come you're not gonna finish that"? Jim inquired. "That's all I smoke" I replied. With that, Jim took the cigar out of the ashtray and laid it in one of the large planters in front of the hotel, but put it discreetly at the rear where it would not be seen. I was a bit puzzled but then Jim said "leave it back there. You don't want to waste it. One of us can smoke it later or tomorrow." And for the next few days, each time we went out to have a *cigar, Jimmy looked in the planter and declared, "It's still in the bush."*

Chapter 7   "Itsa nica place to a eat"

After touring the city on the Greyline bus tour we ended up down in Little Italy. The girls wanted to shop and the guys figured we would just find somewhere to sit and have a beer as Jim was pretty worn out and it was over 90 degrees. I went with the girls at first just to make sure they were headed in the right direction, and then went back and joined Jim and Lee. Shortly thereafter we went down Mulberry Street (the main drag in what is sadly left of Little Italy). We went into one of the restaurants I used to eat at all the time when I spent time in the city. As we sat down, we noticed it was rather warm inside and getting warmer. We asked about the air conditioning and they told us that it was not functioning. After a very short discussion we decided to find another restaurant that did have air. The heat was bad enough but the humidity was 85% and stifling. As we did not want to walk too far, we stopped in at what was soon to become "our favorite place," Positano's.

We were greeted in typical Italian greetings and seated at a mezzanine level table towards the rear of the restaurant. As we all were starving appetizers and bread were in order. Fried Calamari, a little eggplant and an antipasto plate got us started. Jimmy of course went right for the wine. Dinners were shared and we sat delightfully eating and drinking for over two hours. As we were preparing to leave, the owner, Willie, came over and offered us cappuccinos and, better still, some of his special house wine, which we all gladly accepted. Jim the connoisseur made sure the wine was palatable and declared after pouring a large glass for himself, "We can all have just one more before we go." With no schedule whatsoever, we concurred and enjoyed some of the best house wine I ever had. Jim and I went out for a quick cigar, and as we were standing there we started barking for the restaurant, telling people passing by that this is where to eat and convincing them this is the real ticket. We were quite successful and soon the restaurant was filling fast and considering it was only 4:00 in the afternoon Jim was doing a good job.

After "just one more" came a couple of times, we bid farewell to the staff and especially Willie at Positano's, destined to return again. And on the bus ride back, we got to go by the United Nations building and Jim proudly gave them "the middle finger salute."

Chapter 8   "A deal you can't refuse"

One of my favorite restaurants in NY is Carmine's, either uptown or on 44th St. near Times Square. If you ever get to NY, make sure you go. All family style servings.

We sat down at a great table, just the 6 of us. Lee had a hard day and figured "screw it" and said "bring me a double Glenlivet's on the rocks." The rest of us had the norm of wine, martinis and cosmopolitans. We ordered a round of appetizers, a Carmine's salad, anti-pasta platter, and of course, fried calamari.

We were all talking about the day and just having a good time, when they brought out our drinks. We all stared in amazement as Lee's Glenlivet was set on the table. It was in a huge water glass and full to the top! It must have been a third of the entire bottle. Lee just hoisted the glass,

*smiled and said "I believe I just may have two of these."
And of course, he did.*

*Dinner came in waves of brasciole, shrimp and chicken
with more pasta than you could imagine. The appetizers
were gone, drinks on round two, and everybody having a
great dinner. Even Jimmy ate a bit. Dessert was definitely
an option as they have great cannolis (as opposed to
the "flying cannolis" you will learn about later) and
tiramisu to die for. We ordered up a round of desserts
and cappuccinos and admired the atmosphere of all the
famous NY "gentlemen" that adorned the walls.*

Chapter 9   "I'm staying"

*As our tennis tickets included some day and night sessions,
we had quite a bit of flexibility in when we could go. We
were all there really just for Jim and the NY atmosphere,
so we didn't care one way or the other. It was Sunday and
we decided to go to the day event. Hot as hot gets, about
92 degrees and 100% humidity, we headed out to the
tennis complex. We watched a couple of good matches,
and after lunch we went to watch the final day match.
This ended about 4:45 pm and the tour bus leaves the
complex back to the hotel exactly 30 minutes after the last
match of the day session is over, so we were ready to book
when Jim, who had been studying the pairing sheet all
day, decided he wanted to stay for the night match, which
included Martina Hingis and Roger Federer. The girls
were tired, hot and plain worn out, and Lee and I looked
at each other like "oh man, I just want a shower and a
martini." With that, the girls were booking, and Jimmy
said to Mel, "leave all my stuff, I'm staying." Without
a blink she obliged, and Lee and I knew right then we
would be watching the night matches.*

As everyone has to depart the stadium after the last day match and then re-enter for the night match, we decided to (what else) go have a beer. I waited with Jim at the handicap elevator, and Lee took the stairs to meet us at the ground floor. Now this elevator is strictly for the handicapped. Period. As we were waiting in line behind a young gal, pregnant and pushing a stroller, and an elderly couple with one in a wheel chair, the elevator arrived and the attendant stepped out. To our left several rather obese (Jimmy knows I'm being extremely polite here) people started to get on, and the attendant let them! I asked why they were allowed to board first, before the pregnant gal, Jimmy and the elderly couple; second, the elevator is for handicapped people not overeaters; and third; the escalator was 15 feet away from where we were. We were pretty much told to wait for the next elevator, at which time the New York boy in me came out. I went into a tyrannical outburst about the abuses people make of handicap accommodations. If you can walk like they did, you can make it 15 more feet to the escalator. And maybe one or two fewer boxes of Twinkies wouldn't hurt either.

When the elevator finally returned and the doors opened, I took over and escorted the people who really needed to get on the elevator first, getting "if looks could kill" stares from the attendant. I then stepped out and headed for the escalator (practice what you preach, right Jimbo)? When I got to the base the attendant there was helping people off and I asked her about the policy and told her what happened. Her statement: "I saw those fat-asses getting off, and if they tried to get on with me here, they gonna be in for a big surprise. Get your sorry ass over to the escalator I would tell 'em." With that said, Jim declared, "Hallelujah, beer time," and off we went.

The three of us found a great little table in the courtyard by Arthur Ashe stadium, and had a beer and cigar. Of course, as we were getting ready to go back into the stadium, it was time for "just one more."

Once back in the stadium Lee and I were dead dog tired. Jimmy looked as if he were set to run a marathon, and we could not figure out where he got this burst of stamina (must have been the excitement). Jim decided it was time to eat, so we got him organized with a can of food, tube and other paraphernalia. Usually Jim eats via a large suction syringe type device, but in tight quarters he can do this with just a funnel into the feeding tube. As he was eating a young boy sitting next to us was fascinated. Adults stare, but young people are curious. Jim cast him a smile and back to chow.

The best entertainment of the night was these three guys walking up and looking for their seats. They walked up the stairs passed us and then realized they had gone up too far. As they walked down past us the guy in front had a big long trail of toilet paper sticking out the back of his pants. Jim Lee and I just busted out laughing. This was "Saturday Night Live" material. The guys walked down, and then out of sight, with us still howling.

A few minutes later, they returned, and headed across the rows in front of us. And, the lead guy still had the tail of toilet paper stuck in his pants. This in itself was still funny, but what got us really laughing was when Jimmy said, "You think one of his buddies would tell him, wouldn't you?" It put us over the top. People were staring at us wondering what could be so funny.

After the matches ended, and we boarded the bus back to the hotel at 10:30, Lee and I looked at each other and we were glad we stayed. It was a long day but we knew how much it meant to Jim. I still can't believe it to this day that Jimmy held out in that heat for almost 14 hours.

Chapter 10   "Holy Cannoli"

Finding bad Pizza in NY is really hard to do. Finding bad cannolis is just about impossible, but we managed to do it. After returning from the stadium at 11:30 pm we were starving (the girls, however were not. They went back to Carmine's for dinner and a few cosmopolitans). The girls were hanging out in "Club 51," which was deemed the official party room (Robin's and mine which was room 2251). Lee and I booked out in search of food while Jimmy partied with the girls and had some wine. We found a Deli/restaurant that served pizza, so we ordered 2 to go and a couple of cannolis and cheesecakes to go.

After a $100.00 bill for the food (which was surprisingly high even for NY) we were back and ready to dig in. When the pizza was opened it was clear this was not your typical NY pizza. It was almost a doughy bread bowl filled with cheese and meat, and it was pretty bad. We turned our attention to the cannolis. With the first bite we knew they were just as bad as the pizza. For those of you who don't know what a cannoli is, it's a tubular shaped crust, rather firm, filled with a cream made from ricotta cheese and sweets. These were soggy and tasted like the box they came in. Melanie decided these needed to be thrown out, and not in the traditional way. They needed to go out the window. Jimmy concurred. Problem is the windows only open 2 inches. Nonetheless, the cannolis were dispatched through the small opening to a splattering fate below.

Chapter 11   "We're gonna be on TV"

We managed to get tickets to the "Early Morning Show" on CBS through the Steve Furgal's tours, the catch being we had to meet the bus outside the hotel at 5:45 in the morning. Biggest draw was that John McEnroe was the guest that day. We knew Jimmy couldn't make it, but as fate would have it Jim had brought with him and was reading one of McEnroe's books. Jimmy said, "If I could get this autographed that would be awesome."

We got to the show dragging ass from the night before, but the excitement was getting us going. The show started and we all had made the typical tourist signs declaring "Hi Mom" or "We're from Oregon."

Melanie was able to get the attention of Steve who directs the outside operations of the show, and explained Jim's story. Steve said he would make sure the book would get autographed. There were several news stories before John McEnroe came out, but when he did it was cool. As he was waiting fans approached him several times for autographs, and when one fan persisted John… well… became the John we remember and he told the fan where the ball would end up he asked again. At that point Melanie thought that now there was no way John would sign any autographs.

When the show returned to the air John played a few volleys with Dave the weather guy and messed around. At the end he greeted fans on one side of the show area, and Steve flagged us down. He took the book from Melanie and briefed John on the circumstances. John signed the book.

We were all on TV, Jimmy watched us from the comforts of the hotel, and Melanie got the book signed. Steve and John, if you ever happen to read this book, you made one man very happy, and for that we are grateful.

Chapter 12   "Let's go sightseeing and pub crawl around NY"

Pub crawling was Jim's idea, pretty much as everything was on the entire trip. It was the last day of the trip and we all decided to blow off tennis and bum around the city for the day. No planned itinerary, just head on out and see where we ended up.

We headed out down 6th Ave. towards the Chrysler building and Grand Central Station. As we passed the UBS building, Jim just couldn't resist saying hello. So we wheeled up in front of the building and in his greatest humbleness he also bestowed upon them the "middle finger salute." Time for a beer.

We cruised through the lobby of the Chrysler building and then over to Grand Central station. After some photo ops it was time for a beer. After two beers (there can never be just one) we cruised over to the Empire State Building. We had lunch and of course, a beer, and contemplated our next move. Ellen and Melanie had never been up to the observation deck, so Robin took the girls up and the guys went to the bar. Jimmy drank a Margarita… then one more… then half of my beer.

The girls eventually returned and it was mid-afternoon. As we contemplated the next move, Jimmy decided it would be great to go back down to Little Italy for some more of "that great house red wine at Positano's." The girls were ready to shop a bit more on Canal St., and with the prospect of another great Italian dinner in mind, we hopped a couple of taxis and headed back to lower Manhattan.

We arrived in Little Italy a bit too early for dinner, so the girls headed out for some more shopping and Jimmy, Lee and I headed for the bar. We found this small Italian restaurant that was open for cocktails, and Jim didn't complain. It was still hot as heck out, and Jimmy went for a glass of red, Lee a Glenlivet and I had a martini. We were just sitting and talking and commenting on how the bartender was so old he most likely served Al Capone when he was in NY. I left to find the girls and let them know where we were, but most importantly to make reservation at Positano's.

At about 5:30 we headed over to Positano's for another dinner, and Willie and the staff greeted us with open arms. We were seated at the front window table where we had a great view of Mulberry Street and all the action going on in Little Italy. Jimmy decided to go outside and hawk for the restaurant and drum up business for Willie. The rest of us started in on the fabulous house wine that was delivered to the table. I went out to hunt down Jim as he had wandered off (no surprise) and I found him across the street talking to a street artist. I grabbed a cigar and walked over. Jim was trying to commission the young man to do a sketch of the restaurant and was pushing pretty hard. The young man didn't think he had enough time, but Jim convinced him to try anyway. With the artist secured, it was time to eat.

Willie brought us an onslaught of appetizers (we told him "you decide, we'll eat whatever you bring out"). Eggplant, calamari, shrimp, just the best. We were gorging ourselves and the main courses were yet to come. The wine was flowing and Jimmy headed back out to see how the artist was doing and bring in a few more customers.

Dinner was better than we remembered, and it was just a few days ago we were there. Veal paramagian, chicken rottini... it just kept coming. Jim returned and advised the artist was doing fine, and he needed another glass of wine. We were in seventh heaven and just living large. We started to contemplate dessert, and Willie suggested we go a half block to Ferrara's Bakery on the corner.

The masterpiece of the restaurant was completed, and Lee and I slipped the young guy a hundred bucks for the painting. Little did we know (until later) Jimmy also gave him a hundred. I'm sure he was a happy camper, but the painting was worth it. It was fantastic and still hangs in Jimmy's home office. Off to the bakery, where we bought an array of cookies, pastries, and of course cannolis to take back to the hotel. Now, if just one of us is sober enough to get a cab back uptown...

Chapter 13 "Night cap"

We all had to be up early as we had a 6:30 am flight, and Jim does not do mornings well. That did not stop us from going to "Club 51" to devour the black and white cookies, cannolis, and pastries we brought with us. We needed to finish the booze we stocked in the room anyway. Jim, Lee and I decided to go downstairs and have one last cigar, and as we got outside, Jim headed straight for the planter, and yes, the cigar was still there, and no, I never smoked it.

We enjoyed the last night's cigars and headed back up to the club. With the booze nowhere near done, we decided we would leave it for the staff and everyone headed out for bed. We had one more day (albeit a travel day) and we were sorry to have to leave.

Chapter 14   "Are you following us?"

We all met in the hallway at 4:45 in the morning to begin the trek to LaGuardia airport. We manhandled luggage and Jimmy down to the lobby and waited for the limo. As the van pulled up, and the driver got out, we realized it was none other than Vladimir, the driver who brought us here. It must be karma or something. Anyway, Jimmy hopped up front with his buddy and off we went. No tour on the way to the airport, and the ride was quiet. I guess we were all dreaming of the trip and just how special it truly was. The rest is the normal flight home, uneventful, which is the best way to fly.

Summary   "Absolutely the best, bar none"

I have been on many trips in my life. Wonderful places with my lovely wife Robin (Australia, Mexico, anniversary cruise) and family trips I will always hold dear. But this trip will always be the most memorable in my life. We never argued, no one was the leader, and we all just went with the flow. I know that this trip was very special; not just that six great friends were together, but we all got to live the dream Jim so deeply wanted to live. It wasn't about the tennis, the food, and the drinks. None of that mattered. We all bonded to a common heartfelt feeling of being with someone who was so special to us, so great a person that if the trip cost ten times as much no one would have blinked. I have never bonded with people as I did on this trip.

I know none of us will ever forget this trip, and we hope and pray we have the opportunity to go back to NY one more time. Because when we get there, I know we can always have "Just one more"...

It is Peter and Robin who are there when Melanie calls and Jimmy hits a crisis point and needs to be rushed to the hospital. It is Peter and Robin who can always be relied on to make him laugh, put him in his place, or to rub his back and just sit with Jimmy. They are the definition of class and they will be there for Melanie and the girls when Jimmy is gone.

September 18th, 2008
(from Jimmy's website)

Jim's Medical Update
From Melanie

Since my last update, Jim was treated for pneumonia. He is very susceptible now due to his compromised swallowing. He aspirates more and this causes infections in his lungs.

Jim's right leg is failing so he is being fitted for a brace on Thursday, September 18th. It takes a tremendous amount of energy for him to walk because he has to drag his almost useless left leg and now that the right leg is failing, he is falling more and that is not a good thing. The brace will keep him walking.

Even better, Jim's custom built, Notre Dame blue, elevating, circle turning, stop on a dime, go 6mph wheelchair is being delivered Friday, September 26th. We are very excited because this will give Jim so much freedom plus conserve what little energy he has. He will be able to go outside, get the mail, visit with neighbors, and maybe even prune his beautiful roses again!

Jim uses a BiPap-AVAPS machine to help him breathe especially when he is lying down. Because the pressure settings are so high, which makes the pressure very strong, Jim has developed a pressure wound on the bridge of his nose. This is very dangerous as any infection would compromise his health so we are going to the hospital once a week for treatment.

I have been searching for months for a new "mask," one that could withstand the air pressure but not have to be worn so tightly that a sore developed. We tried a new full-face mask last night, it's not perfect but there are no pressure points and it can handle the air pressure. This seems like a lot of work but the only alternative is for Jim to have a tracheotomy and be placed on a ventilator. This procedure is inevitable but we want to put that off as long as possible and as long as it doesn't compromise Jim's health.

I know the above sounds like a lot and, in some respects, it is but Jim is doing well and so am I. My goal is to keep him comfortable and active and so far, he is. Sometimes too active... but always upbeat and positive.

Love to all. Until my next update,

Melanie

Jimmy on Jimmy

While I have tried to talk to many people who were key in Jimmy's life, it is impossible for me to capture the feelings of his friends and families. I have tried to share their words, written perhaps as primitively as mine, but full of honesty and love and sadness.

I asked Jimmy to write a synopsis of his own story. He did so as his health was failing badly. Extended stays in the hospital in October 2008 and late December signaled that the end is near. He made it to his birthday, January 13. He will not make to his next one.

> *In January or February of every year I have a full physical done by my family doctor, Dr. Mark Scherlie. I have been going to him ever since we moved to Salem. We just hit it off. He's my kind of doctor and I feel like we've become friends because of what we've gone through together. In my opinion you couldn't find a better family doctor period.*
>
> *Even though prostate testing for men isn't recommended to start until they turn fifty, I told Mark just after my fortieth birthday that I wanted to start now with prostate tests. My father had prostate cancer. I've had many friends have cancer, and to be honest with you, cancer scares the hell out of me. He said he didn't think it was needed this early especially since I was in such great shape, but since I was the patient he'd do it.*

Now, except for three sports related knee surgeries and a broken arm as a kid I had nothing wrong with me my entire life. From then on I did the prostate test every year as part of my physical. Every year the test results were the same: point 1 (0.1) which is basically nothing.

At my physical in January of 2003, after his feeling around he said my prostate felt a little different but the PSA test was the same, at point 1 (0.1). He said he knew I was the kind of guy that wants closure to everything so he said he was going to send me to a specialist at the hospital even though he didn't think there was absolutely anything to worry about... it was just a precaution.

Dr. Mark sent me to Dr. Elmgren at Salem Hospital, one of the sweetest guys you'd ever want to meet. He redid the test, agreed with Dr. Scherlie and said the only way to be a hundred percent sure is to do a prostate biopsy. Ever had a prostate biopsy? It hurts like hell, and doctors have told me I have one of the highest tolerances of pain they'd ever seen. I had it done, which was no fun at all and waited the two weeks for the results.

Again the doctor thought there was nothing to be alarmed about.

That same year my Uncle Len Hauprich, who was brother to my grandmother Helen on my mother's side, and my best friend, took me to the Masters on Thursday. It was a life's dream come true. We had the best time, just the two of us, and it ranks as one of the greatest days of my life. I barely remembered to call the hospital for the results at the time they said to call, which happened to be right when I was on the course just a couple of hundred yards past the fifteenth green.

Then the shocker. Dr. Elmgren said he couldn't believe it but I indeed had prostate cancer and to call him as soon as I got back to set up an appointment with him and to bring Melanie, my wife, along. I told Uncle Leonard and we went straight to the beer tent. I was scared but knew enough that if it was at the beginning stages. I had a great chance for recovery. Arnold Palmer does commercials about getting checked out. He's always right.

Upon returning to Salem, we went to the appointment and the surprised doctor explained all the different ways prostate cancer can be treated. I asked him what I ask all doctors: "If you were in my shoes what would you do?" He said if you really want to be sure there's only one solution and that is to have what they call a radical operation. If none of the cancer had broken the wall so to speak it's about a ninety-nine point nine percent cure and you're done with it. There can be complications that I won't go into to but I'm the kind of guy that goes for the sure thing and, hey, I was only forty-nine years old. So I had it done, was sore for quite some time but after a year of going back I was officially pronounced cancer-free.

Through the battery of final tests – I was now fifty – one of the tests that isn't done very often is a hepatitis test. Both Dr. Scherlie and Dr. Elmgren said to not be concerned but they were sending me to another specialist at the hospital, Dr. Larry Gates. Another great guy and we got along well. He had done my colonoscopy. He said the only way to be sure is to have a liver biopsy. Oh boy, another biopsy, but again I wanted to be sure, but this one hurt even more than the last one. As luck would have it I was positive and I had the worse kind you could have: Hepatitis C.

Great, now what, I thought, as I believed there was no cure for Hepatitis C. Well there is a cure, but it's an almost unbearable process and extremely expensive. Since mine was the worst kind there is, they have an eleven-month process, instead of six that you can go through, with no guarantees and you just hope that it works. There are severe side effects though because the drugs are so powerful. The worst effect is the possible development of suicidal tendencies. You feel like you have the flu all the time and there are countless other symptoms. And then there's the question that you might go through it all and it still doesn't work.

Hepatitis C... painful therapy... eleven months... little chance for success... Tough choice. Well again I thought that if I can get rid of it I'll only be fifty-one when the treatment is over and I'm a pretty tough guy with a high threshold of pain so I thought, "Here come the Irish!" Let's try it.

For the first two or three months it wasn't that bad, but then things took a rapid turn for the worse. I felt terrible all the time and I had a small case of psoriasis on my elbows for as long as I can remember. Since I wasn't reacting to any of the other bad side effects the "evil gremlins" decided, ah, we have psoriasis, we can attack, and attack they did.

Psoriasis covered my entire body, skin just peeled off, and my whole body was raw. It was as uncomfortable as anything you can imagine. I never had one night of any deep sleep and I honestly thought I might be dying. My doctor, Dr. Gates, when he saw me, took one look at me and said, "That's it, you're done. You have to stop."

I told him I had an appointment with my dermatologist lady the next day and to let me at least go see her first. I thought I've been through almost five months of hell and I really don't want to have to throw it away and stop now.

As if this wasn't all bad enough, on top of all this, Melanie was in San Antonio with my nieces, as her sister was dying with breast cancer. She had no idea what I was going through. I didn't want to tell her as she had other pressures on herself. Besides being in San Antonio she was still working by computer managing a dentist office here in Salem.

By then, I was a sight for sore eyes. I couldn't wear any shoes, barely some wooly socks, so that's what I drove in to go to the appointments. No shoes, just socks. Dr. Hale, the most educated and professional dermatologist around (she has a five month waiting list for new patients) researched what she could and called her mentor at OHSU (Oregon Health and Science University in Portland). She said she would try to find a drug that was worth a try. But it would be a horror story getting it approved by an insurance company.

Dr. Hale's mentor, Dr. Hale, and Dr. Gates used every argument they could to the insurance company. After making it through five months of therapy, I didn't want to throw that time away. I'd gone through way too much pain, agony and suffering for nothing. To make a long story short, the drug worked, which let me continue with the Hepatitis C treatments and I completed the program and was Hepatitis C–free. Not that the next six months weren't hell, but at least my skin wasn't still peeling off.

For the next year I felt great but I did think I was developing a little bit of a slur in my speech toward the middle of the year. All the doctors said it's probably just a side effect from the powerful drugs I was on during the Hepatitis

C treatments (which entailed going to the hospital for a four-hour IV. I also gave myself two shots every week, and about sixteen pills a day). They said in time the side effect of the drugs would wear off. Time passed but the slur did not improve.

At the end of 2006 I asked some of my closest clients if they detected any slur and one said, "Well I called you one night at about 7:00 p.m. and I did detect a little slur, but I thought you just had a glass of wine or something." I asked Melanie the same thing and her answer was the same.

I sensed I had a problem, because the nights they were mentioning, I hadn't had any alcohol to drink.

My annual physical was at the beginning of January as usual with Doctor Scherlie and I brought the slurring thing up to him. The good doctor had been so right on everything else. He said there had been no change in any tests I took. But, sensing my discomfort, he continued. He said that because I talked for a living as a teacher, that maybe I was just a little self-conscious, but he would send me to a neurologist. Still, not to worry. Heard those words before.

The neurologist's name was Doctor Wynn and Dr. Scherlie said he would run some tests. So I went and he ran some tests that hurt like heck and then made a follow up appointment for February 20, 2007. Melanie went with me.

February 20, 2007, "a day which will live in infamy" – for me. What he said was the biggest shock you could ever hear in your life. His diagnosis was that I had ALS. We were both speechless. Melanie started crying, and he said a few things but we really weren't listening. It seemed surreal. We both wouldn't have thought about that in a million years. We both thought he was going to say I needed to take some speech lessons at most. Instead he read me my rights and pronounced my death sentence. In fact we had to make another appointment to ask him questions, as we were in such shock after hearing him the first time. I came home, sat in a chair and we both cried our eyes out.

How could this happen? I had survived so much. Why this? I didn't want to die.

When we went back the biggest question I had was, "How long do I have left?" In his opinion I had the symptoms of the disease for probably a year already. There are different types of the disease and I was diagnosed with Bulbar, which is the worst as it has the shortest life span. In his opinion he said I had approximately six months. That would be normal for a Bulbar diagnosis patient in my condition.

Amyotrophic lateral sclerosis (ALS), often referred to as "Lou Gehrig's disease," is a progressive neurodegenerative disease that affects nerve cells in the brain and the spinal cord. Motor neurons reach from the brain to the spinal cord and from the spinal cord to the muscles throughout the body. The progressive degeneration of the motor neurons in ALS eventually leads to their death. When the motor neurons die, the ability of the brain to initiate and control muscle movement is lost. With voluntary muscle action progressively affected, patients in the later stages of the disease may become totally paralyzed. It is so cruel a disease because you lose all control of your muscle movements, you can't breathe and you die, even though your brain is as sharp as a tack.

Most doctors will tell you it is the cruelest disease there is. At some time in your life you've probably had a discussion with someone that if you could pick, how you want to die? Drowning, catching on fire, plane crashes are all mentioned. Most people say just quickly with no suffering. Well I didn't pick it, but I just heard how I was going to die... the absolute worst way possible. Constant deterioration of my body that no medication, no therapy, no anything can help. It's totally untreatable and there is absolutely no help that can be administered. There is no chance of any recovery at any time of the progression of the disease. It just keeps working on you on a daily basis and just keeps attacking your body.

"Bulbar onset" ALS, which starts in the brain, effects about twenty-five percent of those diagnosed with ALS. The initial symptoms are slurred speech. These patients first notice difficulty speaking clearly. Speech becomes garbled or slurred or a there is a loss of volume frequently. Those are the first symptoms. Difficulty swallowing and loss of tongue mobility follow. Eventually total loss of speech and the inability to protect the airway when swallowing are experienced.

This is exactly what I'd experienced.

It's totally degrading to have the thoughts in your mind and try to converse with people and they just can't understand you. It's as frustrating a feeling as you could ever imagine. Swallowing has been out of the question, I haven't had any solid food in twenty months and will never be able to again. No more juicy steaks, a good pizza, a great hamburger, nothing, zero. The only way I get the needed nourishment is through a tube in my stomach that I have filled at night while I'm sleeping along with a breathing machine so I can breathe. The breathing machine is great but it's as uncomfortable as can be and has put a wound on the top of my nose because of the pressure.

Doctor Wynn highly recommended getting a second opinion from the best he knew on the disease, Dr. Shin-Lou at Oregon Health and Science University (OHSU) in Portland, Oregon. In late March after another battery of tests from Dr. Shin-Lou, he confirmed it. I indeed had ALS. I asked him the same question: "How long?"

His answer was nobody ever knows, that everybody is different and we really can't tell you. I should enjoy life as much as possible. Take the trip you always wanted to take, get your affairs in order and try to have as good as time as you can, doing whatever you want to do, eat and drink whatever you want. (At that time I was able to eat.) Dr. Lou said for some people it's short term; for some it's longer. I could get hit by a bus tomorrow and die before he sees me next, so just live life the to the fullest, and even though it will always be on your mind, try to enjoy the time you have.

The problem was I knew a lot about ALS, as it crossed my lifetime on four occasions with people that I knew or knew of. There was Lou Gehrig who the disease is named after, the Yankee great; I knew it from one of the groomsmen in our wedding, Ty Taylor, who was a co-worker with me in Cincinnati when I worked for Coca-Cola; I knew it from Bryce Bagnall, a client of mine that was a vintner; and I knew it from Bruce Edwards, PGA Championship legendary golfer Tom Watson's long-term caddie (John Feinstein wrote a great book on Tom and Bruce's relationship as caddy, friend and dealing with Bruce's diagnosis and handling of ALS called **Caddy for Life,** *that I highly recommend you read). The results are the same for all diagnosed. It's an ugly, horrendous,* *incurable, little known by the public, terribly under funded disease that wreaks havoc with the patient, their families and their friends. The only difference is the length of time each individual has and nobody can predict that. I can see why some people immediately have thoughts of suicide and continue to do so as things become harder and harder.*

As I said earlier the first stage you go through is absolute total shock. You are completely numb as you've been handed a death sentence that can't be fixed. The second stage is total depression as I had planned so well my retirement years with my loving wife, Melanie, and all the things we were going to enjoy together in contrast to the modest way we had lived our lives. I had two years to go on my job that I loved, helping other business owners with their problems and helping them get on the right track. I had been doing it for sixteen years, declining much higher paying jobs because it was so self gratifying to see these businesses improve and prosper. Believe me, Melanie and I cried a lot. I cried every day at different times of the day whenever the thought hit me… I'm going to die and there isn't anything I can do about it.

My next stage was out and out total anger. I had just gone through two major life-threatening illnesses and survived through good doctors and sheer determination. How could this happen to me and why? I am a devout Christian, and know everything happens for a reason, but for gosh sakes how much can one's faith be tested? Luckily I had a great pastor, Father George Wolf at our church, who had gone through the other two ordeals with me. He told me to just keep the faith, that I was an unbelievably strong person and since I had a heart of gold, I'd be OK.

That helped. I slowly began telling people of my diagnosis, first family, then very close friends and relatives and then little by little other people. It was not easy and some people started treating me differently. Some shied away from me, not knowing what to say. I knew it was tough for a lot of people to take and not just me.

Three months later I was over the aforementioned stages and got back to my old self as much as possible. My three month check up with Dr. Shin Lou at OHSU was coming up and I was in for another battery of tests. They are on call twenty-four hours a day, seven days a week, but only schedule or set-up an appointment every three months to see how your body is doing through the tests. I had the disease. There was nothing I could do about it, and so what's next?

Dr. Shin Lou only sees patients from around the country two days a month. The rest of his time is spent on research. He is one of the most experienced doctors on the disease in the country. I knew patients, especially people that were coming in for their first appointment after being diagnosed, would be in pretty bad shape emotionally. It takes a certain kind of man to face these types of people that have been handed a death sentence and he can't do anything to help them. Talk about frustrating. Dr. Shin Lou is a very proper, Oriental, staid business-like professional doing a job that has to be gut-wrenching. Not exactly a jokester if you know what I mean. But as most people know me I'm different, and after getting over the "stages" I was back to my optimistic, smiling, talkative self to anybody I saw. Why change?

Well, I knew I threw Dr. Shin Lou for a loop when he walked in with his two nurses. I was seated on his chair and facing his computer, got up when he walked in and said Hi Dr. Lou, I'm Doctor Culveyhouse how are you feeling today? I had him sit on the gurney and hit his knees and made them jump up like they do when doctors are testing your reflexes. I faked looking in his ears and asked him, "Well let's see what the tests say," as I went back over and sat in his chair and faked looking at his computer. I thought he was going to fall over laughing. The nurse later told me they had never seen him laugh like that EVER.

That was my start with Dr. Shin Lou and a relationship that developed from that day, just like I had developed relationships with all the other doctors, nurses, blood takers, receptionists and anyone else in the multitude of doctors and hospitals I have been in throughout the last four years. THAT is my style. They see so many depressed people, so many people that complain about everything, so many people that are downright nasty to them and all they are trying to do is help you and make you more comfortable, and try to help cure you. After going through all the results of the tests I asked Dr. Shin Lou that after thinking about it for hours and hours, days and days, I had figured out what a great life I had lived already. There were no big trips I really wanted to go on. In fact, there was nothing I could think of that I really wanted to do differently than the obvious things that I could not do anymore.

Dr. Shin Lou said, "You know, Jim, with your personality you would be the perfect fundraiser for ALS Research." That clicked as I always enjoyed helping people. This disease was obviously near and dear to me. I had people that I was very familiar with that had died from the disease. I knew a lot of people from my golf and business careers. I loved goals and projects to work hard on. I was a very organized person and taught these subjects at the *college. The perfect fit, I thought, and said, "Thanks, Dr. Shin Lou... I'll get back to you."*

Dr. Shin Lou introduced me to everyone in the office, set me up with the MDA-ALS research people and I learned more about the disease, what was and wasn't available and was gung-ho. One small problem, though, I had no funds or budget to start with and my staff was me. That was a problem. "No problem," I said.

I knew I wanted all the funds I raised to go one hundred percent to ALS research, I wanted zero administrative costs unlike almost any other charity and wanted none to go to me. The funds raised were to go strictly to scientists, researchers and doctors that desperately needed money so they could seek to work on a cure. The only little money in the country they receive is from the Defense Department because strangely, more soldiers come home with ALS than the norm and no one knows why. The problem is it's not financially feasible for the pharmaceutical companies to spend millions and millions of dollars on a drug or cure when the life expectancy is so short. It's a losing proposition and I understand that being a businessman. Yes it does seem unfair, but I do understand it and understand their position perfectly. It's not financially sound for their investors or their shareholders. Money has to be raised a different way... through contributions.

I've always been good at problem solving but this was a tough one. Since I had been involved with golf since I was ten (when I started caddying) I thought this was a good place to start. I earned four letters in golf at my high school and was inducted into my High School Hall of Fame. I earned four monograms at Notre Dame and was inducted into the Circle of Honor. I was a pretty fair amateur golfer winning two club championships and various other amateur tournaments. I had served as president of our club and was on the Board of the Junior-Senior State Golf Association. Throughout my golf career I had met a lot of people. I had a computer, I had the information on the disease, I had MDA-ALS as my helpers, time to spare and I decided to give it a go and see how what kind of an impact I could make.

I've played in a summer tournament in August called the DK that is a fun, great tournament run by two great people, Dave and Vicki Lawrence. They have a BBQ every year the night before (and after) the tournament. I asked Dave and Vicki if I could say a few words at the BBQ the night before the tournament. It's a husband and wife gathering so there were a lot of people that didn't know about my diagnosis because I saw some of them only once a year at this tournament.

I've given a lot of speeches in my life and never been nervous but I was nervous that night. I just explained what I had gone through the last four years that many did not know and what I was facing now. When I was finished there wasn't a dry eye around. I did tell them of the fundraising I was going to start and that I would dedicate the rest of my life to it... that I had some MDA-ALS research envelopes that I would leave at the first tee tomorrow at the tournament check-in and if anybody was inclined to donate anything I would appreciate it. To my astonishment almost three thousand dollars was collected. It was a great start. I sent everybody that donated a personal thank you note. That is how my fundraising campaign started and it made me feel good and hopeful.

Alex, my dear sister Shawn's husband, gave me the greatest gift to help me at this point. He had never done it before, had no extra time working a full time job and was teaching extra classes at the University of Nevada Las Vegas at night. He also had a newborn (my Goddaughter Aubree) and a four-year-old (Prescott) and he was trying to finish up the last part of his doctorate. Despite having no time, and no real website experience, Alex built me a website.

My site, www.jimculveyhouse.com shows how kind, passionate, and giving Alex is. He stayed up late many nights just to help me. It sure shows what kind of man my brother-in-law is. One of the happiest days of my life was when my sister married Alex. Shawn and I are eighteen years apart and I adore her. I knew she would be fine for the rest of her life, because he is one good guy!

Alex and I change the site at least once and usually twice a month. This was the tool I needed to get the word out. The power of the internet is staggering and now I could reach friends from other places we lived, past Notre Dame Alumni and monogram winners and even my high school friends as well as old clients and friends we had. This is what's made this campaign take off. It's a domino effect as I ask in every email if they would please pass the site on to their friends, relatives and people on their contact list. I still send a personal thank you note to every single person that contributes even the six children that have donated, four of them for one dollar. (This is the minimum on the site so anyone can donate something.)

I then started sending emails and letters to all my computer contacts and golfers that I knew including some clubs where the pros would help me get the letter out to their members. During the winter, Dana Londin, our PGA head professional at our club, Creekside Golf Club, worked with my wife Melanie, without me knowing about it, on holding a fun, fan friendly tournament for local pros who would secure pledges from the members at their clubs and have all the money donated to my fund for ALS research. I was proud as MDA-ALS designated me as Oregon State Spokesperson for MDA-ALS research. Of all the people I had to tell that I was diagnosed with ALS, Dana Londin, was one of the toughest. I knew he'd take it pretty hard. We had been close since he became our pro and had more than a few matches against each other.

Dana and Melanie finally told me of their plans and we started planning along with the heads of the PGA section here in Oregon. The best man in our wedding, Jim Terry, a VP for Coca-Cola sponsored the event. On April 30, 2008, we kicked off May, which is ALS Awareness Month, with our "nine pro shootout." It was a typical Oregon April day, a little cool, a little rain and a little wind, but fun was had by all. The great news: thanks to Dana's idea and hard work, the day netted close to twenty-three thousand dollars. A beautiful crystal trophy was given to the winner and to my surprise Dana announced the winner only gets to keep the trophy for a year because this was to become an annual event to kickoff ALS Awareness Month on my behalf every year.

All the pros also showed their class, commitment and generosity by donating their winnings to the fund and promising to bring another pro next year to make it twice as big. What can you say? Thank you seems like not enough, but again as I reiterate over and over again, the more you give, the more you get in return.

John Lindley

One of the groomsmen in Jimmy's wedding party developed ALS and passed away several years ago. At the time, while certainly considering it tragic, Jim was not moved enough to learn more or reach out to him. Much changes when "it happens to you."

Despite his advanced stage in the progression of the disease, Jimmy is always willing to try to help new patients whose lives have been shattered by those three letters, ALS. One of those is John Lindley. Despite the fact that Jimmy's ALS was so advanced at the time that he could not be understood speaking, he used his computer to reach out to recently diagnosed patients like John Lindley to encourage them to keep moving forward.

At the recent fund raiser held at Creekside, Jimmy encouraged John to come as noted in the e-mail below.

> *John –*
>
> *I'm so happy that you will be able to make it. If you have your tube put in the 28th you'll be fine by the 30th. Let's hope for a nice day. The schedule includes a free pro clinic at 12:30 p.m. on the range. At about 1:20ish we will have pictures and short greetings and a short speech by me that my wife will give as I'm too hard to understand.*

I have made you John Lindley, Mickey Riley and me as Honorary Chairpersons of the event. Pam is going to caddy for Sean in Mickey's honor. (I had another gentleman from the Parks Dept. who had to retire last year when he was diagnosed but I don't think he'll make it as his buddies say he wouldn't feel comfortable.) I'll mention him anyway as Mickey won't be there either as he lives in Australia. The Shoot Out will start at 2:00 p.m. Hopefully the media will cover it but you never know, I've tried with Channel 12, KYKN and the Statesman Journal. We'll see.

Now for the important stuff. What type of ALS do you have? Unfortunately I have bulbar, the same as Tom Watson's caddie, Bruce Edwards. I only use my feeding tube once a day, when I go to bed and it feeds me while I'm sleeping with all the needed nutrients for the day. I also use a breathing machine while I'm sleeping. I haven't had anything to eat in over a year.

Who are you seeing? What doctors and where? When were you diagnosed? Fill me in. Maybe I can share some things with you. Because of my fundraising efforts I've met a lot of the experts and places to get help and answers. They made me Oregon State Chairperson for the MDA-ALS division and I was selected as one of the 31 people across the country to be honored each day in the month of May for May ALS awareness month. (My day is May 13th.) I've dedicated the rest of my life to do two things, raise awareness for the disease and raise money for research. I work pretty hard at it and have just passed $250,000 by a strictly grass roots effort by myself from my computer and my website that my brother in law did for me. You should check it out: www.jimculveyhouse.com. It's very informative and I update it regularly. As a golfer you'll love the last update and I urge people to pass it on to their contacts. I personally thank every person that gives a donation no matter how small it is, even the four children who gave $1 which is the minimum through the site.

I look forward to meeting you. Just ask Keith Banks, your pro at Illahe how you can make a pledge. He's a good man and I appreciate his commitment to this endeavor. See you on the 30th.

Respectfully,
Jim Culveyhouse

October 28th, 2008

(from Jimmy's website)

Medical update from Melanie Culveyhouse

On Monday, October 6th, Jim was admitted to the Salem Hospital for what we thought was a mild case of pneumonia. We were instructed by his pulmonologist, Dr. John Silver, to go to the emergency room and have them evaluate Jim. By the time we got him to the emergency room Jim was in respiratory distress; I knew we were safe because we were in the hospital, but I was really scared. Emergency staff put him on his BiPap/AVAPS machine which assisted his breathing and allowed the doctor to get his heart rate down and his oxygen levels up.

Many tests were done and lots of antibiotics were given those first two days. Dr. Silver told us Tuesday night "it was time for a 'trach' to be placed." Because Jim's lungs are compromised by ALS, placing a tube in his trachea *opens his airway and allows him to breathe on his own or on a ventilator.*

A tracheotomy was done on Thursday, October 9th, by Dr. Nicole Vander Hayden, a trauma surgeon at Salem Hospital . She was wonderful!! From surgery, Jim was placed on a ventilator and sent to ICU. In ICU the goal was to get Jim off the ventilator during the day and only use it at night while sleeping. The first two days that worked great – then the bottom fell out!

Jim started to decline and decline fast. He was unresponsive and his vitals were the pits. I have to admit I thought we were losing him on Monday, October 13th. As we later found out Jim not only had a very severe case of pneumonia, he was battling sepsis (sepsis has been dubbed the medical "perfect storm" because it is a medical crisis that can attack patients who are fighting off even seemingly nonfatal illnesses or injuries). Severe sepsis killed Muppets creator Jim Henson, who had been hospitalized for pneumonia, and recently took the life of actor Christopher Reeve, who was being treated for pressure sores of the skin. With this insidious illness, the body attacks itself. Bacteria inside the body may grow out of control or invade the body from the outside through wounds or IV lines. Sepsis is not an infection; it is a systemic inflammatory response syndrome to an infection, which poses dire risk of organ damage and death and kidney failure (due to the sepsis).

By Tuesday night, October 14th, Jim was showing signs of improvement but he was very disoriented and delusional from the disease and medications. On Wednesday, I had not slept at the hospital and I arrived that morning at 7:30. The respirator therapist came in at 8:00 for Jim's normal treatments. He turned to walk out of the room; I was standing at the bedside holding Jim's hand. Before the respiratory (our hero Mike Phillips) therapist got to the door Jim starting struggling to breathe and his oxygen saturation levels again fell like a rock. Mike acted with great care and precision in getting the appropriate help for Jim. Mike called for Dr. Silver. When Dr. Silver arrived he assessed the situation and cleared the room of unnecessary people and started to work on Jim. A mucous plug had lodged in Jim's airway (Dr. Silver said to tell Jim it was the size of a golf ball) and it needed to be cleared. It took LOTS of medication to calm Jim down, so he rested most of that day. When I was explaining what happened to my family, it was like a scene out of the television show ER. It was like a perfectly choreographed dance; everyone knew what to do and when.

After Wednesday, Jim steadily improved. We were told a date of Oct. 23rd was the target date for release. In order for Jim to be released from the hospital, all caregivers had to learn to take care of his "new" medical needs. We attended classes and passed our 24 hour test (we had to care for Jim for 24 hours.) Last Thursday Jim was sent home in an ambulance accompanied by two very pretty blond, female paramedics!!

We've been home five days and Jim continues to regain his strength. The ventilator is going well and we are creating a new "normal" around our house.

As many of you know, Jim and I have a very strong faith in Our Lord, Jesus Christ. He was with us at every turn. The care and the people He placed in our path were nothing short of a miracle. We felt every prayer and witnessed God's power and mercy first hand.

Jim and I want to thank you for the many prayers and calls of concern. We especially want to thank my sisters Dee and Melinda and our friends Robin and Peter who spent numerous hours by our side in the hospital and with our family helping to keep things going.

Much love to all,
Melanie

November 28th, 2008

(from Jimmy's website)

Melanie has updated you all on the month I kind of missed, October 2008. When I say missed – people could see me, my eyes were open, but five minutes later I could not tell you they were there or what was said. It's a pretty scary feeling and to go through it for eighteen days you do wonder if that's just the way it's going to be because if it was some decisions needed to be made. But constant patience from loving life Melanie, reassurance from one of our best friends Robin Juhren and the passionate spirituality of my sister-in-law Dee who were all my "sitters," I finally "came back!" Trust, faith, and prayer – good things to pass some time away.

Go Irish!

In the last sixteen months, through Jim's efforts, more than three hundred thousand dollars has been raised to support ALS research. Jim has sent scores of letters to all of the contacts he has made over the years. A diligent planner, no stone is unturned when an opportunity presents itself. Whether it is golf tournaments, dinners or any type of fund raiser, Jim coordinates all the planning to ensure the goals are met.

Moreover, anyone who has made a contribution to ALS through Jim's website receives a personal note back from Stump. While it is difficult to hold his head up and only a ventilator keeps him breathing, the under-sized son of James Robert Culveyhouse perseveres.

While committed to his ALS fund raising efforts, Jim also has his own kind of "bucket list" – a term made famous in the recent Jack Nicholson/Morgan Freeman movie of the same name. When given the news they each had incurable diseases which would soon take their lives, they compiled a list of things they want to do before they "kicked the bucket."

Jimmy has his own bucket list. After being diagnosed with ALS and getting over the shock of it, Jimmy had a fundamental decision to make. With anywhere from six months to a year left to live, he could either fold his tent and shield the world from what would become symptoms that would make many turn away, or he could fight – fight for those who don't have the disease yet- fight to help find a cure.

It has been more than two years since Jimmy was diagnosed with ALS. He has fought and defied all odds and Melanie has been with him every step of the way.

At the top of Jimmy's "bucket list" is to raise one million dollars for ALS research. His life the past twenty-four months has been focused on that goal and he is one third of the way there.

One of the items on his list was related to his family. He wanted to make one more trip with Melanie to see his sister Shawn, brother-in-law Alex Herzog and their two children, Aubree and Prescott, as well as to play a couple of rounds of golf. While still very incomplete emotionally with the relationship he has with his father, Jim also wanted to reach out to his mom and dad one last time.

Last spring, his golf goal was checked off the list. Though barely able to talk and with his gait now noticeably impaired, incapable of holding his head upright for more than seconds at a time and unable to eat food other than through a tube in his chest, Jimmy played a round of golf with his good friend Mez and played all eighteen holes. Jim shot ninety-nine – and we aren't talking about a par three course. We are talking a resort course that people pay a lot of money to play. We are talking more than 6,500 yards from "the blues."

Time with Shawn, Alex and the kids has been blissful for Jimmy. His kid sister, some eighteen years younger, has become one of his closet friends, as has her husband Alex. Alex has been tireless in his support of his brother-in-law. While Jimmy knows a lot about planning, his relationship to computers was somewhat limited. Alex is very familiar with computers. When the news that Jim had ALS hit with Jim's subsequent decision to try to raise one million dollars, Alex knew that the most efficient way to do so was to develop a website. He had never created one before, but he was ready to learn.

If you totaled up the hours Alex has spent developing Jim's website and updating it, he could have had a part-time job. But Alex has the same kind of respect and affection for Jimmy as do so many others. Jim has been a mentor to Alex in so many ways. His business and teaching experience have helped Alex immeasurably in his duties at the University of Las Vegas, Nevada (UNLV) and now as a Dean at the University of Eastern Utah.

Meeting Alex at a restaurant in the Mandalay Bay casino for breakfast, Alex is quick to give praise to Jimmy. "He has been like a big brother to me," exclaimed Alex, who went on to speak with admiration about the courage Jim has displayed.

With Alex's help, fund raising for ALS research has gone well, but Jimmy is fighting to get those with the resources to give more.

January 7th, 2009

(from Jimmy's website)

Medical update from "Nurse" Melanie

We hope everyone had great holidays and a very Happy New Year. Jim and I had a wonderful Christmas surrounded by lots of family and friends.

Very early Sunday, December 28th Jim was having difficulty breathing, a temperature of 100.4° F, and very thick secretions. We tried all the usual treatments but he was lethargic and I knew something was not right.

I called our good friends the Juhren's at 5:30 a.m. and asked if they would help me get him to the hospital.

The one good thing about being on a ventilator is when you enter the emergency room you are taken to a doctor ASAP. They did the usual tests, asked the usual questions and determined he had an infection somewhere. The emergency room doctor was top notch and started Jim immediately on the "big gun" antibiotics.

Jim was admitted to the hospital and we were moved to the fourth floor, PCU... our "home away from home." Fortunately, Evelyn was our nurse (she was one of the nurses who cared for Jim in October) and Amy "Donald Trump" was the Charge Nurse. They greeted us with warm affection and although glad to see us they were sorry it had to be in the hospital.

Dr. "Midnight" Silver, our hero, determined Jim had pneumonia and needed to stay for four to five days to get IV antibiotics. On Monday afternoon (I had just left to go home after twenty-eight or so hours) Jim had a mucous plug and went into respiratory distress. They moved him to ICU so he could be monitored more closely. He stayed in ICU until Wednesday night (they moved us at 10:00 p.m.). We were happy because he couldn't go home if he was in ICU.

We wanted to be released on New Year's Eve Day but ole' Doc Midnight said no. We had a great New Year's Eve with lots of friends and champagne! Jim was released, reluctantly, by Dr. Silver and we came home New Year's Day. Jim is doing well at home. We have been fighting bronchitis/pneumonia since Jim left the hospital in October. I think he needed one more heavy duty round of medications to get rid of it and he did.

The doctors tried to get Jim off the ventilator during the day and he did great in the hospital lying in bed, doing nothing. However, being home and being active does not allow him to breathe on his own. But that's OK. That is why we have a ventilator!

Jim has a follow-up appointment tomorrow; this should tell us a lot about his health and what we can do to avoid these hospital stays. Please continue praying for us, we feel them and God hears them.

Love to all,
Melanie

Two days later, Jimmy regained the strength to write, typing on a lap-top while on a ventilator. He continued fighting to give

January 9th, 2009
(from Jimmy's website)

Dear Friends,

Hope you had Happy Holidays and are off to a great 2009! Even though it was a tough health year for me it was also an extremely rewarding year. First of all, my little grass roots campaign has now collected $300,401.50 donated by 493 people, including ten children who also received a thank you note as I do for every single person who donates. The rewarding part was to see how generous some people can be.

Equally rewarding was hearing from so many people in my past as far back as grade school and meeting new people from all over the world. The power of the Web has helped tremendously when people see my website (thanks

to my brother-in law Alex). They tell their family, friends and contacts to look it over and how they know me. All I can say is thanks and keep doing it, and I'm eternally grateful to all of you. God bless you all.

The problem continues that few people know about the disease. It's why I'm dedicating the rest of the life I have left, as Oregon State chairperson for the MDA-ALS Research division to help change that with all of your help getting the word out and passing my website on to family, friends and your contacts. It's informative, amusing in parts and we change it about once a month so you should bookmark it. You know my lifelong mission statement – the more you give to others, the more you will receive back.

Now I don't need any more scares like the eighteen days in October, where I had a few close calls because my lungs are compromised by my ALS. I needed a tracheotomy which is when they placed a tube in my trachea which opens the airways and allows me to breathe on my own (for a very short time) or on a ventilator. I had the premier Doctor in the world do it, Dr. Nicole Vander Hayden. Having all the "other" things to contend with you would think it was a big challenge. Not for her! Some people probably like me better like this because I can't talk at all. But they need to be beware that I have a computer machine that I'm going to start practicing on so that it will let me speak (different voice) but at least I can communicate. I really do feel more empathy for deaf people; it's been as frustrating as hell, one of the hardest things I've ever had to do. Mentally it drives you nuts. Try it sometime for one day and you'll see what I mean.

Now I know that most of you forgot that my birthday is Tuesday January 13 and you've probably forgotten to get me something. Don't call me at the last minute to go out to breakfast, lunch or dinner. Although a nice gesture, I haven't eaten anything solid in almost two years. I've got something I want from all of you that is so very inexpensive that every single person that receives this new update will be able to afford. It won't change your lifestyle at all. I want you to give up that one extra Starbucks, half of the cigarettes or cigars you smoke, to have a bag lunch today instead of going out. Skip that paid movie Tuesday night, skip the car wash... it will probably rain anyway, and you can think of countless others in the same category. And you ask what category is that – it's the five-dollar category. I'm asking you to give up something that costs you about five dollars for one day for my birthday and... Go to my website at www.jimculveyhouse.com and donate five dollars (or more if you feel really generous).

OR

Call Gavin Johnson's office, the Regional Director for MDA-ALS at 971-244-1290 and phone in your donation. Now I'm counting on everybody to get behind this. I've been extremely lucky. I have exceeded my original timeline diagnosis by more than double but with these last two scares, I'm also a realist and know it could happen any day at any time. It's the mystery of this awful disease. Soooo... I want to make my fifty-fifth birthday the best ever by receiving the most donations ever (I know east coast people it will take longer).

God bless everyone,
Jim Culveyhouse (and Melanie)

I had committed to Jimmy I would complete his story in time for him to be able to read it himself. Time was running short.

I was wrapping up this book as I learned Jimmy went back into the hospital with serious issues. This represented the third time Jimmy had been hospitalized since October. He is on a ventilator now and he continues to weaken. His mind has started to play games with him and Jimmy started to forget things. He continues to battle but I thought I better get his story done. So I finished what I had written and the week of February the first. I sent the first third of the book to Jimmy, who was still able to type in e-mails. He expressed excitement to be reading it. Then I heard nothing. That is when I called Melanie and heard he had been rushed to the hospital.

I took the liberty of forwarding e-mails with the draft to several people, including many of my ND buddies previously mentioned. I confessed to all I had no knowledge about writing and sought assistance in editing. I think I was also in search of some kind of validation that I had not totally messed up the story of a dying man who put his faith and trust in me.

After reading my e-mail, one of my buddies, Frank Murnane responded and suggested I contact Mike Bonifer, one of our classmates. He mentioned "Bonnie" was in LA, totally into the Hollywood producing and consulting thing and he had even taught at Notre Dame. Eager to seek assistance, I e-mailed Bonnie.

Mike Bonifer, one of my favorites: Mr. Bookstore Basketball in 1973. Bookstore Basketball was born at Notre Dame when we were there. In the spring after varsity hoops were complete, a tournament was founded to find the best five-man team on campus from among the students. Basic rules: five on five, half court, call your own fouls, no substitutes, first one to twenty-one wins and advances. One and done. If you lose you are out. Location of tournament: the asphalt hoop courts located behind the university bookstore.

The first year, 1972, was the year before Jimmy entered ND. There were no restrictions placed on who could be on what team. As a result, the team of varsity hoop players, John Shumate, Dwight Clay, Gary Brokaw, I think Peter Crotty, and quarterback Cliff Brown, beat a team in the finals that included fellow hoopsters Goose Novak, Geek Wolbeck, Jerry Samaniego, myself, and I forget the other player. After that, they limited the teams to one varsity player.

In 1973, Jimmy's freshman year, a team led by Mike Bonifer, quarterback Tom Clements, tackle Steve Sylvester, Norb Scheckel and another football player, the late John Dubinetski, won it all. Bonnie was the 1973 MVP. That same year, Jimmy was on the same Bookstore team as football Hall of Famer Joe Montana, who was quite a hoop player too.

Like Jimmy, after doing a lot of other things, Bonnie found teaching. He is now a consultant, teaching businesses, like Jimmy, with a course called "Improvisation for Business." He has also written a terrific book entitled: *"Game Changers"*

While Bonnie confessed book editing was not really his thing, he asked if I knew that Pete Demmerle had died from ALS too?

I was stunned. Pete Demmerle? Class of '75? First team All American wide receiver at Notre Dame, academic All American, postgraduate scholar, only one of six players in the history of Notre Dame to receive those three honors and play on a national championship team? That Pete Demmerle died of ALS and I didn't know it?

I Googled his name and read his story in utter shock. A successful insurance lawyer with a beautiful wife and four lovely daughters, Pete was diagnosed with ALS in 1999 and died May 24, 2007. What rock had I been living under those seven years when he and his family lived their own ALS nightmare?

I did not hear about it at reunions, or when I got together with my ND football buddies from my class, 1974. I did not read about it in ND alumni or Monogram Club communications. I just didn't know. And if someone had told me, it sure must have gone in one ear and out the other. I just didn't know and I felt sick about it.

I also did not know that another Notre Dame football All American from one of the greatest ND teams ever has ALS as well. Pete Duranko, who was on the Irish 1966 national championship team, the last ND team to win the title until Demmerle's did in 1973, also has ALS. Duranko is in his sixties now and has been a tireless advocate for fundraising and ALS research while battling the illness in his home state of Pennsylvania.

The reason for my elevated distress was that I was now engaged in understanding more about ALS. I understood the horrors of the disease. I was writing a book about Jimmy and had come face to face with how little I had done since the loss of my brothers to Huntington's, or the loss of my friend George Maly of Wellesley, or my father, step-mom, sister in law, JoAnne Carlson and my wife to cancer. I had been paralyzed. Cancer and neuro-muscular diseases had impacted my family in a big way and I had done nothing.

After reading about Pete, I felt the need to reach out to his wife Kate, first to express my condolences and second, to let her know about Jimmy. I also reached out to Dave "Ghost" Casper who had been very supportive of his former teammate since he had been diagnosed. Ghost had visited Pete when he was sick several times and had made it possible for Pete to make the trip to Canton, Ohio, when Casper was inducted into the Pro Football Hall of Fame. He was quoted in the internet article I read.

Pete and I were not close at Notre Dame probably because he hung out in places with which I wasn't familiar, like the library.

But I should have known. I always thought he was one of the best of all time, and a good guy. I should have known.

I had forgotten about Pete. Ghost had not.

Bonnie had not forgotten about Pete either. He gave me a link to a YouTube video of him and his friend, Geoff Ratte, visiting Pete a few years ago. I opened the video, and there was Pete, sitting behind a voice assistant machine called a synthesizer which allowed him to "talk" to visitors since he was incapable of doing so on his own. If you Google "Pete Demmerle," you can see it. You can also watch Pete scoring the two point conversion in ND's twenty-four–twenty-three win over Alabama. Number eighty-one was special.

In watching the first video, all I could think of was how hard this must have been for Pete. Geoff and Bonnie, who recorded the video, made Pete laugh as hard as I am sure he had laughed in a long time. It is basically bathroom humor, the kind of which guys at Notre Dame laughed at in the old days. But the video moved me also as I thought about Jimmy and the difficult phases he has had to endure.

I had forgotten about Pete. Bonnie and Geoff had not.

I reached out to Ghost, seeking assistance to connect with Pete's wife. Forty percent of Jimmy's wedding party had ALS. The coincidence of two record-breaking varsity athletes who were at Notre Dame also having ALS at the same time was overwhelming. Notre Dame has an enrollment of less than ten thousand. ALS strikes an average of one in a hundred thousand. What are the odds of ALS striking both Pete and Jimmy, and Pete Duranko, and perhaps other ND students I don't even know about? Professor Curme, my Stats professor, would have to help me on this.

Time was of the essence. Jimmy was in the hospital. I had not heard from Melanie since I sent her the draft. I needed to finish the book, but I had to try to connect with Pete's wife Kate, so I called and left a couple of messages.

Pete Demmerle... Friday the 13th

Coincidentally, I had to drive through Greenwich, Connecticut, where the Demmerle family lives on my way to and from a business meeting in Philadelphia. My first calls from the previous day had gone unreturned.

When I arose on Friday, I thought I am sure I rambled on so much in my message Kate must have thought she had a certifiable whack job on her hands. I decided to try one more time. I thought Jimmy would not have given up so easily. Kate answered the phone and after a few minutes, agreed that on my way back, if she could, she would meet me for a cup of coffee.

Greenwich Connecticut is where the Demmerle family settled. A consensus All-American his senior year at ND, Pete was looking at a potential pro career as a first round pick. He was smart and fearless and had hands that caught anything thrown in his area code.

For the younger generation, Wes Welker of the New England Patriots is a good image of the type of player Pete was. His patterns were disciplined, his cuts were decisive and like a Timex watch, Pete would "take a licking and just keep on ticking." Pete was a coach's dream and he was one of Jimmy's favorite players.

The Irish won the national championship his junior year. Pete was invaluable in the twenty-four–twenty-three win in the Sugar Bowl against Alabama as he hauled in three passes in the first quarter including a key two-point conversion. Tom Clements loved having Pete and Casper as his primary pass options.

In his senior year, Pete caught forty-three passes and achieved deserved widespread acclaim. During the Irish Bowl win against Bear Bryant's Crimson Tide, Demmerle suffered a devastating knee injury, which essentially ended his football career. Could he have toughed it out and made a comeback? Maybe. But Pete had other options.

What Notre Dame taught both Pete and Jimmy, and I guess all of us athletes is that there is going to come a time when you hang up the cleats or "sneaks." Maybe a knee injury will cut short your career or maybe you will go on, like Dave Casper, Pete's dorm mate at Sorin Hall, and become the greatest tight end to ever play the game.

But one day, you will have to join the civilians and you had better have options.

Jimmy went to work for E&J Gallo Winery, and Pete enrolled in Fordham Law School, graduated with honors and began to climb the ladder with the prestigious law firm, LeBoeuf, Lamb, Greene and MacRae, L.L.P. In 1981, he married a beautiful fellow lawyer, Kate LaFleche.

I won't detail the entire impressive scrapbook of accomplishments Pete achieved, which included achieving partner status and eventually being transferred to London, where he was instrumental in saving the well-known insurer, Lloyds of London. Pete was a whiz in insurance law and during the second phase of his life, he prepared well to be able to enjoy his life with his wife, Kate, and their four daughters, Cara, Alice, Tess and Nina.

But ALS does not seek out only the disadvantaged. It is indiscriminant. I think for some reason it searches out the best and brightest on whom to impose its will. Like Jimmy, Pete would not enjoy the golden years with his family.

Kate met me at the Starbucks at the corner of Arch St. and Greenwich Ave. in downtown Greenwich. I was keenly aware it was Friday the 13th. Though not particularly superstitious, when I awoke that morning, I read of the first commercial airlines crash in two and one half years involving fatalities. Fifty people died in the Buffalo area after a tragic accident.

I also learned that morning that one of my high school buddies was rushed into emergency surgery with apparent serious brain tumors.

Joe Roberts, multi-millionaire, philanthropist, and loyal St. John's High classmate has given millions to charities and worthy causes. At the age of fifty-six, Joe is in for the battle of his life. He may not be able to enjoy his golden years either. It made me think that every day during Jimmy's sickness and every day that Pete was ill, it was Friday the 13th for Melanie and Kate.

It was with those two sobering thoughts that I secured a table at the corner coffee house.

Kate walked in and we greeted each other a bit awkwardly. She ordered from the barista and we settled into our table. After expressing my condolences for her loss and my apology for my never knowing about Pete's illness, we began talking about Jimmy and then we turned to Pete.

Pete was diagnosed in 1999 at the height of his career with fourteen and pre-teen daughters. The news for Pete and Kate was devastating as it was for Jimmy and Mel. Pete's diagnosis: Bulbar ALS.

About a year into the illness, Pete lost all ability to converse orally. Speech assistance machinery was ordered and as his ALS advanced, so did the sophistication of the equipment.

At first, Pete and Kate were able to communicate clearly. Pete could type out quickly what he needed to say and little was left to either translation or interpretation. If Kate did not understand, Pete was able to quickly correct her.

We then joked that it seems inevitable however that in relationships men are usually wrong, to which I responded, "So tell me, Kate, if a man says something and a woman can't hear him… is he still wrong?"

And with that, Kate laughed and smiled one of the great smiles where her whole face let go. "Yes," she emphatically responded. I wondered how many times Kate had been able to laugh since Pete died.

We then shared more details about both of our losses and Jimmy's situation and what Melanie must be feeling. Jimmy is now on a ventilator and there are challenges with it as the machine attempts to maintain the appropriate flow of oxygen to the lungs of its patient. A lot can go wrong with a ventilator. Kate knows. Pete was on one for a long time.

Tubes become detached, batteries run low, power outages occur. Mistakes can be made.

When an ALS patient goes on a ventilator, communication is limited. The primary caregiver is left to guess what the patient is feeling. With the knowledge that no matter how sick the patient is, he or she still has total sense of feeling and is mentally aware of everything, the primary caregiver is on a twenty-four-hour vigil to try to anticipate what might be endangering the patient. The Devil assuredly invented this disease.

The process is exhausting. Patients must often be "suctioned" of excess phlegm building in the lungs. The only distress signal may be a bulging of the eyes, or that the skin begins to turn blue or the patient blacks out.

What happens when this occurs at 4:00 a.m.? What happens when you finally take a little break and your daughter is on first call or a caregiver or another family member who may not know all the signs and symptoms? What if they don't have the same instincts and the ability to anticipate?

Simply put, ALS not only drains the life out of the victim. It tests the fortitude of the love and commitment of the entire family.

After seven years of agonizing, humiliating, and thoroughly involuntary atrophy of what used to be taut, finely tuned muscles and mind, Pete Demmerle – All-American, successful attorney, devoted husband, father of four precious girls whom he adored and wanted to take care of – vacated this earthly prison of a body to join Lou Gehrig and others on May 24th, 2007. Finally, it was his time.

But Pete, too, spent his life as an ALS patient "fighting to give." After he was diagnosed, Pete, like Jimmy, like Pete Duranko, committed himself to raising money to fight this disease. He was an amazing advocate and helped raise literally millions of dollars to help find a cure. The Notre Dame and business circles around him rallied to do what they could. Pete never asked for credit; he only asked for support to find a cure.

Pete was an active member of the Connecticut ALS chapter searching for ways to increase funding. He traveled to Washington, D.C., to lobby on behalf of ALS. Pete was a winner his entire life, but never were his competitive instincts more in evidence than after he was diagnosed and he made his mind to fight ALS and never give in.

I loved the movie *Ghost*. Patrick Swayze dies and yet he is able to somehow connect with his grieving wife. Ironically, Swayze is now ill and he won't enjoy his golden years, it seems, either as pancreatic cancer is ravaging his body.

But in *Ghost*, even after death, he loves his wife and misses her so. He wants to connect with her to tell her he loves her. There are some people who believe they can communicate with the deceased. It made me think about what Pete would say:

"Kate, I love you. Thank you for loving me. Thank you for giving up your law practice to support our girls and me. I am so sorry for how hard this was for you, but thank you. Cara, Alice, Tessa, Nina, I am so proud of you and I am so sorry to not be there for you. Thank you for taking care of me. You have to know, I would do anything to just be there to see your smiling faces, to give you the chance 'to dance with your father again.' I love you, Kate. I love you, Cara. I love you, Alice. I love you, Tessa. I love you, Nina. I always will."

"Dance With My Father Again" – the late Luther Vandross. I cry every time I hear it. I think about how my sons feel about their mom, about how my daughter feels. I cannot listen to that song. When it comes on, I am done.

I cannot imagine either how Cara, Alice, Tess and Nina feel, or Sarah or Pari, or Kate or Melanie. They will only be able to enjoy that dance in their dreams.

Pete did not want to go. He loved just being in the same room as Kate and the girls. But it wasn't his choice. I can only imagine him looking at his beautiful wife and wishing that he could hold her, to let her know how much he appreciated her love. She could have left. She did not. She loved him. The girls loved their dad. They stuck by and tended to Pete during the hardest of times. This was and is what love is about.

This was Friday the 13th. My guess is, Pete would be scheming to do something special for Kate on Valentine's Day. He would probably act as if he forgot, and then it would become apparent that not only had he not forgotten, he had gone out of his way to make Kate feel special.

Sound familiar? Pebble Beach… the Lakers…front row seats… trying to think of something that would make his wife feel special… that was what Jimmy has always been all about, from Cincinnati, to Washington, to Salem, Oregon. He has always known he has not been the easiest guy with whom to live. But he knew if it were not for Melanie, his life would have been so much different. I am sure Pete felt the same way about Kate.

Before I left, Kate reflected a bit. After tending to Pete for seven years, it was hard to move forward. Tending to the every physical and emotional need of the man you love dulls the senses. She mentions that it seems even harder in the second year as she is able to better reflect on the good times and what life would be like today with Pete as her partner. Morning swims give her time to reflect and the energy to keep moving forward. She has her girls, assists other families with health issues, but ALS took its toll on Kate, too.

ALS does not just strike the victim. It attacks the entire family. Kate and Melanie know that well. Melanie is in the middle of what may be the worst of times. Near the end, she knows, Jimmy is still fighting to give. But care-giving in the latter stages of ALS may be the hardest thing a spouse will ever do. "Giving up" are two words he could never pronounce. He can't communicate verbally now, but I think Mel knows in her heart, Jimmy wanted to make it to the second anniversary of his diagnosis and he did.

Doctors attending to him have no idea where he finds the inner resolve to keep battling. Jimmy could pass away any day now. By all rights, it could have happened in October when his body was attacked by sepsis. It could have happened in December when he developed pneumonia. Mez visited Jimmy at the end of January and felt it could happen at any time then. But Jimmy keeps fighting.

February 21st, 2009

Well, he made it. I had not heard from Jimmy for a couple of days. Then I received an e-mail from him. He had passed the two year mark of his initial diagnosis.

After sending the initial drafts to some friends to help with editing, one friend, Carol Ensley, donated a thousand dollars to ALS on Jimmy's website. Carol works for a company that has recently announced a string of lay-offs that affected every level of the corporation. Yet, still, she donated. If he has the strength, I know Jimmy will send Carol a note of thanks.

Late last night, I received the following from Stump forwarding an e-mail from one of my ND buddies who read the draft:

> *Stump,*
>
> *Loz here. I was known to throw a few down in Corby's.*
>
> *Hawk has kept us up to date on your battle with ALS. Your willingness to fight on is a true testament to your*

character and, of course, the true spirit of the FIGHTING IRISH.

As a high school math teacher and assistant football coach, I am constantly asked questions about my time at ND. Everyone wants to hear about the 'super stars', championships, etc. I will entertain them with some stories, but I always steer the conversation to the unsung heroes of our time at ND...Al Sondej, Duke Scales, etc.

I want them to understand the true meaning of hard work, determination, setting and chasing goals, sacrifice and so on. As I read Hawk's book during our Feb. vacation, I realized I have another example to present to my students and athletes. You are an inspiration to everyone.

Keep up the good fight.
Go Irish!
Loz
Dennis Lozzi, ND '74
1973 National Champions

Hearing from someone like Loz gives Jimmy new energy to keep fighting. He reads the e-mail from Loz and sends him a long thank you note for making a donation. He then bounces me back with an e-mail:

I'm hangin, but I ain't goin down Til I'm ready to go down and it ain't time yet, got some thongs to close up.

Typing has become very hard but his spirit seems to propel him through another day of pain and suffering, yet another hospital crisis.

March 5th 2009

I had to travel to Portland on business and it afforded me the opportunity to see Jimmy one last time. When I booked the flight,
three weeks prior, I thought I would be going to pay my respects
to Melanie. Jimmy's last visit to the hospital brought him as close
to death as ever. But somehow, he rallied. I would get to see my
friend one last time.

In my brief meeting with Kate Demmerle, I really got the sense of
how devastating the disease is on family members near the end.
For fighters like Jimmy and Pete, they keep battling to live, ignoring the option of picking "the day."

Many ALS patients near the end of their lives choose the day that
they want to die. Once on ventilators or when they become totally
immobile, they choose a day when they end not only their pain
and suffering but that of their families as well. Tired of watching
loved ones change their feeding tubes, administer the Nebulizer
or humiliated for the final time of having their backside wiped by
a loved one after a bowel movement, they pick a day to turn out
the lights.

The strain on the family of an ALS patient near the end of life
is almost unbearable. Melanie had to take a three-day break just
prior to my pulling into Pawnee Circle the evening of March 5th.
Her sisters, Melinda and Dee, had left their homes in Texas and
Ohio to come and help Melanie, to give her a break from the non-
stop caretaking.

I did not know what I would find when I walked through the door.
My vision was one of Jimmy lying in bed, immobile trying to type
an e-mail with pencil in his mouth. What I found shocked me al-

most as much as the dream I described at the beginning of the book.

Jimmy was sitting in a motorized wheel chair equipped with an attachable tray. In front of him lay a folder with a draft of the book. When he heard me enter, he raised his arms like Rocky atop of the steps of the Museum of Art in Philadelphia.

My proverbial jaw hit the floor. All I could exclaim was, "You gotta be kidding me!"

Jimmy struggled to rise, almost pulling his ventilator out of his throat. He somehow managed and I was able to embrace this bionic mass of tubes and humanity. He smiled with a sense of accomplishment and settled back into his throne.

Melanie just shrugged and related that the doctors can't believe it. They did not think he would make it through a year after the diagnosis was confirmed. Jimmy had just passed his two year "death date" and he had survived three serious episodes requiring hospitalization. He just wasn't ready to go. He had more money he wanted to raise and he wanted to read his story. He was waiting for me.

When the lungs stop working in ALS patients, they must go on a ventilator, which controls their breathing. They must receive frequent doses of water poured by their caretaker into their feeding tube to keep them hydrated. They must receive frequent Nebulizer treatments to remove excess phlegm from their lungs. They often sit with a hand towel in their mouths to catch the frequent drooling. They are at the complete mercy of their caretakers.

Jimmy still had use of his arms. We met for a while that evening and I told him that after I finished my business in the morning I would be over to see him. He scribbled on a piece of paper that he wanted to go over the book, page by page. He showed me that he had almost finished the draft and that there were too many mistakes. We had work to do!

After a restless night and attending to my appointment, I headed back to Pawnee Circle.

When I arrived, Melanie and a nurse caretaker, Gloria, were tending to Jimmy's morning needs. The longer a patient lives, the more complicated the care given becomes. Jimmy finally emerged in his wheelchair and Melanie got him settled, plugging in his ventilator, providing him with his drool towel and responding to several beeps from a buzzer Jimmy rings when he needs something.

For the caregiver, that buzzer becomes the most annoying sound they hear. It often is rung for the seemingly most mundane of reasons: turn on the TV, turn up the volume, scratch my back, I am thirsty, I have to go to the bathroom – all the little things that occur in a day. But you never know when the ring means something more serious.

Friends come over for dinner that evening. After Jimmy and I finish our review of the book, I leave and attend to more business issues. When I return, Peter and Robin Juhren and their son Kyle are there, along with Lee and Ellen Vaterlaus, and Steve Viale and his wife, JoAnne. Melanie has somehow found the time to prepare another amazing meal and all of the adults are enjoying a cocktail. Peter and Robin's older son drops in later.

Jimmy wheels in and positions his wheelchair between the kitchen, the dining area, and the family room. He "parks his car" and just listens to the wonderful banter of friends around him. There are a lot of jokes, many at Jimmy's expense, and he loves them. Melanie leaves and goes to the bedroom to fetch me some photos for the book. Her absence from the group is extended, partly from fatigue, partly from sadness.

Melanie knows the end is near. Her sadness is coupled with exhaustion from the constant care. She is not the same lively, spirited woman I remember from my last visit when Jimmy still was relatively independent. The constant caretaking has taken its toll on her spirit. Memories of my visit with Kate Demmerle surface. Melanie has had to numb her feelings just as Kate did in the latter stages of taking care of Pete. It is clear to me Melanie does not think she can take much more.

We talk about "the day."

The man she loved has changed so much since their twenty-fifth wedding anniversary almost a year ago. Three trips to the hospital to bring him back to life. All of the other emergencies she has needed to deal with and the constant caregiving challenge her will. Jimmy will choose "the day" and the torture will be over. Melanie doesn't know what to feel anymore so she tries not to feel at all. Jimmy is calling the shots but she is doing the work and it is the hardest work of her life.

By the time this book is printed, I am pretty sure Jimmy will have chosen his day. He does not want to leave. As Pete Demmerle just enjoyed sitting in the room near his girls and Kate, you can see Jimmy loves that same sense of belonging. He weeps openly when I read to him an edit to properly recognize Nick Thiros and the dad Nick really was to him.

At times that night, I looked into Jimmy's eyes and tried to think about what he was feeling. In one of his "Jimmy Updates," he concluded it with, "Boy, this ALS sucks." So when I got back to my room that night, I wrote a poem that is in the back called "This ALS Sucks." I wrote it as if I was Jimmy, looking at everyone he loves, unable to speak but still totally able to feel everything including the fear of "the day." It is in the back of the book along with another poem I wrote Jimmy about his life called, "What a Ride."

I left that night believing that I most probably will not see Jimmy again in this world. I will never forget his eyes when I hugged him good-bye. He has changed my life just as he helped change the lives of so many people he met along his amazing ride. ALS will take his life. I want him to die in peace. He has fought the good fight and he can sleep well knowing he made a difference in my life and all those he touched.

I was pleased to see the announcement by Major League Baseball that baseball has stepped up to the plate in a big way. "Baseball 4 ALS" is a theme that will echo throughout all ballparks this year. There will be ample opportunities to donate at stadiums leading up to Independence Day. Every home team, before the first pitch, will reenact the speech that Lou Gehrig gave on the Appreciation Day held for him at Yankee Stadium seventy years ago on July 4th.

Ever the class act, not even ALS could get the Iron Man down as he uttered those memorable words:

"For the past two weeks you have been reading about a bad break I got. Yet today I consider myself the luckiest man on the face of the earth. I have been in ballparks for seventeen years and have never received anything but kindness and encouragement from you fans."

You might question how Bud Selig has handled the whole steroid issue, but no one can fault him for his commitment to support ALS research. Curt Schilling and his wife Shondra have also been strong advocates for ALS. It is great to see baseball go to bat for Jimmy and other ALS victims.

By buying and reading this book, you have made a contribution to ALS and on behalf of Jimmy, Pete, Pete Duranko and all of the patients and families afflicted with this disease, I want to say, "Thank you."

I had lost contact with Jimmy during the fall. I went through some personal challenges of my own and went to the dark side into a hole of pity from which emersion was very difficult. Two computer crashes and the stupidity of improperly backed up files forced me to re-write most of the book – twice. I didn't have the heart to tell Jimmy that the mistake of this past summer when I lost the file with the entire book… happened again. Jimmy never would have been so stupid.

He has lived a great life. He lived his wild side. He lived the era of obsession with work. He learned tough lessons in the first third of his life gaining wisdom through hard work, perseverance and a commitment to always do his best.

In the second third of his life, he climbed the ladder at Gallo and Coke before settling into a community in Salem, Oregon, where he could teach and inspire those around him. A man of incredible faith, he has remained loyal to his loving wife. In adopting his nieces, Sarah and Pari, he has breathed new life into the children he was never able to have.

Jimmy will leave this world soon and join the Iron Man, Bruce Edwards, Pete Demmerle, Professor Schwartz and all those ALS victims who have passed before him, but he will also leave his legacy. Through his efforts, others will benefit. He has been a fighter all his life. ALS will take his life, but it did not win. Not even close.

John Wooden, the great UCLA basketball coach, proclaimed, "Success is peace of mind from knowing that you've done your very best to be the best you can possibly become."

Jimmy Culveyhouse should have peace of mind. He is a proud benchmark for courage by which any other person who develops this horrible disease could be measured. Paraphrasing the words of NC State basketball coach, Jim Valvano, who died of cancer, I am sure Jimmy is feeling:

"ALS may take my body, but it cannot touch my mind… it cannot touch my spirit. Don't give up… don't ever give up."

I love you, Stump. In the words of the old Irish proverb:

May the road rise up to meet you
May the wind be at your back
May the sun shine warm upon your face
And the rains fall soft upon your fields
And, until we meet again
May God hold you in the palm of His hand

Epilogue

I had six goals in writing this book. The first is to raise awareness of ALS. If anyone buys this book, all of the proceeds will go to research support for ALS and other neuromuscular diseases. My goal is to support Stump's efforts to raise at least one million dollars for ALS research in his name. He has helped raise more than three hundred thousand dollars already. Maybe you will not just buy and read the book, maybe you will buy one for a friend, or just make a donation. You can always go to www.jimculveyhouse.com and give.

After achieving the ALS goal, if the book does well, the donations will be split between ALS and cancer research.

Second, I hope you found Stump's life is worth reading about. I am so sick of people who have done bad things who then write books and make a lot of money profiting from them spewing about their "born again" state. The money made from those books either goes toward paying off legal bills about their misgivings, or, worse, to line their pockets. When someone gets caught doing something untoward, why do we support their sins by financing their retirement? The people who profit from *this* book may be your son, daughter, or someone else close to you.

Many diseases have been cured through research, and if not cured, remedies are discovered which can dramatically ease the pain and burden of victims. Because of research funding and hard work some diseases that used to kill rarely do anymore. Polio, tuberculosis, small pox – they all had their day, but not anymore. Stump has the same dream about ALS. It may not help him, but it may prevent someone in your family from getting it.

Which brings me to the third reason: this is a book for you, with what I hope you will agree are some inspirational stories that may positively impact your life. It is about a guy you can admire, a man who is committed to his wife, a guy who has consistently done the extraordinary. Someone said, "There are three kinds of people in this world: people who make things happen, people who watch things happen, and people who wonder what happened." This is a book about someone who just brings joy to others, who, despite a lot of trials and tribulations along the way in his life, just made things happen. We can learn from Stump, from his mistakes, from his successes, and from his courage.

Fourth, this book is dedicated to those in my life who have died of cancer or neuromuscular diseases: for my late wife, Marian, and my cousin Roger and Joan Corke and all my friends I mentioned. It is also dedicated to my Pinehurst golfing buddy, the original "Barrett House boy," Gary Knutson, who died of colon cancer a couple of years ago. He was a fighter too. And it is for my dad, Edwin Stevens, who died of pancreatic cancer, and his wife, my step-mom, and cancer victim, Lucy Stevens. "Miss Lucy" was to me like Nana was to Stump, just the classiest lady I had ever known. Finally, it is for Marita McBride who died of lung cancer the summer before her daughter Marian passed away.

This book is also for my biological mother, Marilyn Cain Stevens, and both of my brothers, Jeff and Ned. All three died of Huntington's Disease, a neurological murderous sibling of ALS.

I did not know my mom. After I was born to her, I was put into foster homes because she was schizophrenic and in a mental institution. We never had a relationship and I so regret that. Both of my older brothers and I grew up in some difficult foster home circumstances. Our respective childhoods read like a Lifetime movie script.

We never knew our mom had the killer Huntington's gene in her system. When her body began the dramatic involuntary twitching and her speech became so slurred and her gait so unstable, she was misdiagnosed. Everyone around her thought it was just a reaction to all the Thorazine and Lithium she had ingested in the halls of St Elizabeth's mental institution in Washington, D.C. But my mom did not have "tardive dyskenesia," the name given to the chorea like symptoms she manifested; she had Huntington's.

It was not until my middle brother, Ned, was diagnosed with Huntington's Disease that my oldest brother Jeff and I realized we were also at risk to get the gene. As we quickly learned, with Huntington's Disease, also called Huntington's Chorea, if you get the gene, you get the disease. And like ALS, if you get the disease, it is a death sentence.

Ironically, Jeff knew a lot about Huntington's. He was in the music business and he knew that the great country singer Woody Guthrie died of Huntington's. Jeff became a voracious reader of the illness. He even sought out Woody's widow and his famous son, Arlo. He just wanted to learn as much about it as he could. I chose to ignore it, to act as if it wasn't there. With the exception of my visits to the mental institution to visit Ned where I would be visibly confronted with Ned's disturbing symptoms, I just blocked it out. I had a wife to tend to, a start-up company to help run, and five beautiful kids to raise.

There are tests that can be run on your blood today that can determine whether or not you have the Huntington's gene. I helped one of Ned's illegitimate children, Michele, get tested after she spent ten years trying to track down her biological parents. Imagine the euphoria of finally finding your biological father, only to learn he had a horrible genetic disease. Fortunately, the tests confirmed she doesn't have the gene.

Failing to see the sense in learning in advance of the gloom that would await me with a positive result, I chose not to be tested. I told all of my children that if they ever want me to get tested, I would do it in a heartbeat for them. They have no interest in the test either.

Despite his educational commitment to becoming a walking encyclopedia about the disease, Jeff never got tested either.

Any child of a parent who has Huntington's has a fifty-fifty shot at getting the gene. With Ned already diagnosed with it, my brother Jeff and I were hopeful – no, we were confident that we dodged the bullet that was lodged in Ned's DNA. Would we avoid the gene that killed our mom and that was sucking the life of our other brother in his early fifties?

Huntington's beat the fifty-fifty odds. At least two thirds of the Stevens brothers would get the disease. I think I have beaten the odds. Jeff did not.

I mentioned Jeff was a musician. And he was a gifted one. Growing up in the wonderful folk-rock era of the 1960s, Jeff played the guitar, self-taught, on the farm that was one of our foster homes growing up, in the Catskill Mountains of New York. He eventually would move to California where he would play guitar with Mimi Farina, sister of the legendary Joan Baez. He also worked with Jesse Colin-Young and the Youngbloods, often opening for them in their sold-out concerts. All of the flower children in the crowd and eventually millions others would rock to one of Jesse's songs which became an anthem for the Woodstock generation with the memorable lyrics, "C'mon people now, smile on your brother, everybody get together, try to love one another right now."

Jeff changed his name to Jeffree Cain and actually ended up recording two albums on the Raccoon label, "For You" and "Whispering Thunder." You should check them out. They are vinyl. I actually found them on the internet and bought a couple of them.

Whenever Jeff would visit he would always bring his guitar and play for the kids. When he arrived at my home in the Boston area in 2002, it was the same thing: funny stories to tell, wearing pretty much the same clothes on his back, and always a song to sing.

I noticed it from the first moment he walked in. Jeffrey always kind of sidled along when he walked. Never a fan of exercise, time and an affinity for larger meals had rewarded him with a rather healthy bulge above his belt. But the weight gain should not have altered his swagger so definitively. Jeff was definitely listing to the port side. As he approached for one of his famous hugs, all I could see were the vacant eyes of my brother Ned whom I had just seen two weeks before in the hospital. And when he smiled and spoke his pet name to his youngest brother, "Hi Chrissy," all doubt was removed.

My other brother had Huntington's too. And, ironically, it would kill him faster than it did Ned.

Less than two years later, on New Year's Eve, 2003, Jeff died in my arms in a hospital in Denver. While Ned had been diagnosed earlier, the disease tortured him for twelve more months before he expired in a hospital in California in January 2005. Tragically sandwiched in between, six months after Jeff's death and six months before Ned's was the shocking death of my wife of twenty-seven years, Marian, in July 2004. Marian did not get to enjoy the third trimester of her life. Neither did Knute, my mom, my brothers, or Pete, and neither will Jimmy.

My late sister-in-law JoAnne Carlson won't be able to enjoy her life either.

After Marian died, I never thought I would ever marry again. I never thought I would love again. And I thought no one would ever have any interest in a big fat dumpy guy, a widower with five kids.

Then I met Trice.

Trice is short for Patrice. As loving a person as I could imagine Trice had been married before but never had kids. She learned of Marian's death and offered her condolences. After a few months, we had coffee and I got to know how special she was. We got married and I felt not only was I blessed to find someone, but the kids would have a woman in their lives who would love them unconditionally.... and she has.

It is not easy stepping into an established family with five kids still grieving the loss of their mom, but Trice did it with grace and humility. If there is a more thoughtful unselfish person on this planet, I have yet to meet that individual.

Shortly after we were married, Trice's 55 year old sister, JoAnne Carlson, began showing signs of a digestive disorder. Her energy diminished and her symptoms escalated. In the spring of 2007, just after Jimmy was diagnosed with ALS, Jo was diagnosed with pancreatic cancer. What a shock. How could this beautiful, artistically gifted woman who always took care of herself have cancer? Untreatable cancer at that..

Trice left her work to return to Illinois to join her other sisters, Jan and Laurie in taking care of Jo that spring. Six weeks later, Jo was gone. This year, Trice quit her job again to travel home for another challenge; her sister Jan was diagnosed with a brain tumor and had to have surgery. She has come through it well. But in my mind, Trice joins Melanie and Kate as a person willing to do whatever it takes to tend to the needs of those she loves.

The fifth reason for writing this book is to say "Thank you Trice"... for loving my children as if they were your own.

Tragedy has struck our family. I have given individually to try to help find a cure for the killers of loved family members. But I have been struggling with a way to do more. Many suggested I write a book of our family's tragic story, but candidly, I didn't fashion myself as much of a writer and besides, I just didn't know where to begin. Some of the abusive foster homes we were in, the Huntington's story, the cancer, which also took my father two days before one of my sons was born... I concluded, "Who wants to read about my family's scrapbook?" I didn't know what to do. Then I received the e-mail from Gasman.

I heard about Stump having ALS and I reached out to him. I sent him some things that were meant to be encouraging including a motivational speech I had given to a local high school. He called and said, "Hawk, you've got to write my book." I tried to bail but then it hit me that this might be a way I could give something on behalf of my family and on behalf of Jimmy.

I had already read Mitch Albom's book as well as John Feinstein's and they really moved me, and made me think of my own family.

Someday I may write a book about my family, but after one conversation with Jim and hearing of his life, I thought my story can wait; his cannot. In writing this book and hopefully raising money for research, maybe I can give something back to Jim, something back to my loving, faithful late wife, something to the mom I never knew and the brothers who were robbed of life. I am fifty-six and in the third trimester of my life. I don't know if I have the gene – but if I do, I will know soon and every dollar raised for neuromuscular research may help me or my kids.

Finally, this is a book for Stump. My goal was to complete it in some form before he dies, at least in its rough form. It has allowed Stump to read about his life, not just from my words, but from the memories of those closest to him – his wife, his friends, his students, and from business associates.

So, Jimmy, even though I am not a writer, this book is for you. Soon, I know you are going to pick "the day." Just know, you have impacted so many lives along the way. You are an inspiration to all you touch. Your road has not been an easy one and you are nearing the end, but I hope you can feel the pride that you have made a difference in people's lives, and your legacy of "Fighting to Give" will live long after you have passed from this earth.

Rest well my friend. You lived more in fifty-five years than most do in a lifetime.

Love ya, Bro.

This ALS Sucks

As I lay here thinking about all the things that I
would love to see
I get excited about traveling and watching Sarah
and Pari be all that they can be
And when I think of how I'd go to the Masters and
spend a few hard-earned bucks
I get dizzy, start to get weary and am reminded, boy
this ALS sucks

I dream of all the walks I'd take with Melanie, the
kids or friends I love so dear
And I think of tail-gaiting at an Oregon game and
relaxing with a beer
Or perhaps just get out and tend to my roses... is
that asking way too much?
But I'm limited to just thinking and dreaming
because this ALS sucks

I read my cards and remember well every memory
with family and friends
And I am grateful for those I have not seen for a
while and getting to make amends
I would just once more love to get a chance to have
a party with all and just once more wear a tux
And then I remember I can't walk or talk anymore
I know that this ALS sucks

So blessed to have the blessings of my priest and
the thoughtfulness of all
Melanie, her sisters and my friends have tended to
my needs, I'm driving them off the wall
The kids are helping cook and clean, even learning
how to use the Electrolux
But I would do those jobs and more if I could, boy
oh boy, this ALS sucks

Now I have seen with my eyes what devastation that
ALS has done to a few others I know
And I appreciate more than ever the loving support
that friends and family on me bestow
I have been hoping for a miracle cure or perhaps
just a little Irish luck
So I can beat this thing and then look back and say
to ALS, "Boy, you really suck!"

I had hoped at OSHU that research from the
dollars I raised would maybe find a cure
But now I am too weak and fading fast, the end is
near for me I'm sure
And it is hard laying here with all my thoughts
frustrated at my current state of flux
Praying that I will get better somehow some way,
you have no idea how this ALS sucks

To those like Mom and Dad who don't get to see or
talk to me as often as they think right
Just know I think and pray for all of you each day
and every night
And thoughts of you pass by my window just like
passing cars and passing trucks
I'll see you and give you hugs on the other side and
talk about how this ALS sucks

I wish I could get out of this bed and tee it up at
Creekside, I'd hit my driver out so far
Then I will put the top down and go for a ride with
Mel and the kids in a new convertible car
Then I will hold my head high and shout to the sky
just like the chicken clucks
And say I am done with this disease, I beat you, you
Devil, boy this ALS sucks

And as I fight to try to keep my strength I think of
what you all can do
To help find a cure for this dreaded disease that's a
lot worse than the Asian Flu
Give to www.jimculveyhouse.com and donate to
ALS if you can spare the bucks
And like in the movie *Network*, lean out your
window and yell, "Boy, this ALS sucks"

I love my Sarah and Pari, Shawn, Alex and kids,
Melanie don't you worry about me
I am grateful for what you and everyone else did to
take care of me so tenderly
I have tried to be a good dad and husband and
enjoy life and along the way enjoy a few yucks
And I love you all and I always will even though this
ALS sucks

Your Amazing Ride

Now I'm not much for writing in this
technological age
You just tap out an e-mail or sending a quick text
is the newest communication rage
But when Gasman sent me that e-mail last year and
to which I quickly replied
I contacted Jimmy and learned his life has been
quite an amazing ride

It had been thirty-five years since the two of us had
initially connected
Little did we know how much our lives by muscle
diseases would be affected
You told me about your task to raise a million
dollars with great pride
And this was your mission on a life that has been
on one amazing ride

I met the people so special to you or on whose lives
you've much impacted
To write your story would require some time and it
could not be protracted
The more I looked, the more I learned,
the more I realized
That your life should be shared so that more can
enjoy your life, an amazing ride

Life is filled with many examples of a David slaying
the giant
To not accept "No" when uttered so often you've
been often bravely defiant
Your athletic skills, your giving heart, that Cheshire
grin so snide
The fun you've had, the fun you've created for all
on this amazing ride

The Wizard of Oz taught us to judge a man by how
much that he's loved by all
It doesn't matter when he trips but rather how he
rebounds after the fall
Your courage inspires those who love you, in your
life, Jim, you may take pride
I hope this book will inspire others to give as you
gave throughout your amazing ride

Soon you will sleep and not be in pain and you will
enjoy a courtside seat
And watch over Melanie, Sarah and Pari, Jim I'm
sure won't miss a beat
To keep us all inspired to achieve your dream,
you'll continue to be our guide
God bless you, Jimmy, thank you for inviting us to
be a part of your life, an amazing ride

"Love You, Bro'"

3078725